THE INTELLIGENCE OF

HAPPINESS

How to Thrive Using Authenticity,

Self-Alignment and Simple Neuropsychology

GI GI O'BRIEN

THE INTELLIGENCE OF HAPPINESS
How to Thrive Using Authenticity, Self-Alignment and
Simple Neuropsychology

ISBN   978-1-5445-2311-8 *Hardcover*
      978-1-5445-2310-1 *Paperback*
      978-1-5445-2309-5 *Ebook*

To the pain that made this book so powerful
and to the ones lost by their own hand,
thank you for teaching me.

Most of all, to you, dear reader,
I hope this book will bring relief. May you
put it to good use and delight in
a ravishingly full life.

ACKNOWLEDGMENTS

I would like to thank these people for supporting me through the most testing and transformative stages of my life, for being the light on the darkest days. Without loving me and letting me lean on you, I would not have completed this work.

Thank you John N. O'Brien, Mary Hazel Rudder, John A. O'Brien, Hannelore O'Brien, Asabi O'Brien, Daniel Atwell, Samantha Laverick, Briar Rose-Kershaw, James Inniss, Leandra Barrow, Peter Raftopoulos, Carlo Davids, Alexander Whalmann, Adam Picker, Josh Forrow, Bryce Jones, Celeste Finn, Chanelle King-Morris, Corey Bessener, Jono Horne, Bianca Knotter, Karianne Bail-Lancee, Mike Paseornek, Elliott Barrow, Christine Harris, Cori Lathan, Ariel Phillips, and Dorian Pryce.

You were all a part of this journey in a meaningful way. I'm deeply grateful.

Thank you.

CONTENTS

INTRODUCTION

How much bleach do you have to drink for it to kill you?

Just days before the moment I asked myself that question while sitting alone in my apartment, I actually considered myself to be a happy person. It made me realize I was yet to figure out just what happiness is.

I felt ambushed by this suicidal thinking; it was an excruciating loop of negative thoughts that rendered my Self-worth as nonexistent. I was feeling disconnected from the whole world, angered by its capacity to be so selfish, so heartless, so conniving.

I had the highest of hopes and dreams for my life, rooted in improving humanity and making a meaningful impact. I was one of those people who knew we could be better and do better by each other, and by our planet. How could someone rooted in so much kindness and such great vision be in a stare-off with a 121 oz. bottle of bleach? Would it be enough to kill me? Could I get all of it down? What if it didn't work and I survived, only to have destroyed my poor esophagus? The thought of not enjoying the taste of food couldn't even sway me into any faint memory of pleasure. I had no recollection of better times. When I wasn't choking on ambition, I was suffocating in pain, until eventually I was breathing in numbness, exhausted.

I moved into this small and dated space nestled at the bottom of my childhood home, and truthfully, I loved it. I was grateful to have a place to call my own after years of just visiting home in Barbados, staying in a room littered graciously with others' belongings. Sometimes, for months, I lived out of a suitcase as I worked between Bali, Australia, and Los Angeles—always in transit flights and never truly rooted. I just trailblazed ambitiously into the next evolved state of goals without ever feeling any significant wins. I was chasing the rabbit in loops of Self-discovery, catapulting into new industries with confidence, fearlessness, and a willingness to rise to any challenge.

Right now, I am far removed from that woman.

Right now, my world revolves around reacclimating myself into society. We cautiously ease out of lockdown into what some might praise as reclaimed liberation. Here I sit in contemplation, looking at my belongings, most of which are still packed from moving, and I am seriously considering taking my life. I feel physically tormented by pain I can't properly rationalize, and even worse, I am wondering how the ending of my story could be least burdensome for my family. My packed belongings are among the few things I can recognize with positive acknowledgement. You would assume the thought of how your remaining family members would feel upon your death would be reason to live, but I had no such feelings.

At this moment, I am completely consumed by my disheartened world view. I am unable to see my place in the world, and I don't have a damn clue as to how I let my mind reach such darkness.

I am a shell of a human.

I feel hollow in places where there used to be hope, and I feel everything is loud when I am just sitting blank in silence.

I never wanted to live my life the way it was taught to be lived. My unconventional approach and ambitions too big for my own good may have set me up for my own Self-detriment. For my whole life, I guess in some capacity I was always failing to meet my own Self-set expectations. High performance meant worth. Without reaching for the stars, I wasn't worth the glaze of a shining spotlight. I was in darkness if I was not in the gracious light of achievement.

I place little value on the mindful experience and joys of life in these suicidal moments. I forget that to be human is to feel, to breathe is to live, to have life is to still have opportunity. I forget all the positive affirmations that I advocated hundreds of times and recommended to others. The rationality of what I have to be grateful for does little to snap me out of this place.

So, I write a letter.

That kind of letter.

My last energy is used to construct sentences from lead-weighted words as I purge my soul, secretly hoping someone would care enough to intervene.

How did I end up here?

For a brief moment, it makes sense why I feel the way I feel. I get what I am feeling, and I get why I am feeling it, but even with that understanding, I am lost for hope.

I lose my Self as my dreams fade against the backdrop of a world in crisis. I forgot to be happy and instead strived for greatness. I forgot I was enough just as I am, because everyone kept asking, what's next?

I forgot that happiness happens when nothing else happens, because it is a choice to feel it.

I pick up and put down my phone at least one hundred times. I don't even know where to start to reach out to someone—there's a high-voltage electric fence between me and anyone who could help.

Every time I want to open the gate of the fence, I feel myself dripping in water, drowning in fear, believing I would electrocute myself if I made a single move.

I stay stagnant, a hostage to my Self.

I cradle back and forth in the seesaw of pain and numbness, into tasteless oblivion.

It's a feeling I never want to experience again, ever.

You may not have been pushed to this limit, but in many ways you have felt the pain of being your Self. You are why I wrote this book. We are going to dig deep into what happiness truly is, because if you don't know what it is, you might mistake it for something else, and I never want you to end up in that place.

We grow in the misconception of happiness in so many ways: from success, to lifestyle, to possession. If you expected to be happy because of your income, your life's security, and your employment or relationship status but something is still missing, then you are in the right place. If you are not sure about your core values, belief systems, and all the elements that curate your expectations, then this will be a riveting awakening. Even if you keep falling short of meeting your expectations and find your Self disappointed with some of your decisions, there is a transformation awaiting that will upgrade your habits and behavior. I am going to teach you how your expectations and experience can be aligned so you will feel like you have finally found that missing piece. You can relieve your Self of disappointment and feel like you are the person you have always known you could become. You will feel complete, you will know your Self, and you will love being completely your Self.

I've been mentally and physically abused and bounced back, but was overcoming adversity happiness? I've reached the top of the continent in performance in my role with a multinational corporation, but was success happiness? I've grieved gracefully when I've lost loved ones, but was that grace actually happiness? I did what I had to do when my marriage broke down and I healed from domestic violence, but was that strength and resilience happiness?

I am now an expert in the intelligence of happiness, and here's a little secret: it does not come from circumstance, but rather, Self-concept. Even when life tests you, you can maintain your happiness by discovering your authentic Self. That is the start of freedom and fascination. Every single day, you can indulge in the uniqueness of you being your true Self.

This book will liberate you from comparing your Self to others and from that thing that cuts you deep—comparing your Self to what you think you should have been by now. The expectation of explosive growth and comparing your Self to what you think you should have to show for it can be sickening. Trust me when I say this: alignment is the cure. And even when shit inevitably hits the fan, you will know how to get back to happy, with or without reaching your larger-than-life goals. It's a relief when you can lift the weight of the world and all its expectations from your shoulders. Damn, it feels great!

The irony is, when you surrender, you unlock the secret to what life and happiness are all about, and then you begin to manifest magical things that feel like they just fall into place.

However, things don't just fall into place: *you fall into alignment*.

When you feel the aligned Self, you won't want to be anything else. I can't tell you how excited I am for you to start this journey of opening your Self to the choices and power that come with seeing and perceiving your life in ways that serve your joy.

You will develop Self-awareness and be able to celebrate your evolution. You will see clearly how far you have come, even if it isn't the journey you set out on. I will teach you about the part of your Self that feels (Affective), the part of your Self that thinks and knows (Cognitive), and the part of your Self that can do what you once thought was impossible (Executive).

Embrace the fact that we are all still growing. We are still evolving. We are all constantly improving, and if we are lucky, we become what we focus on.

If every single thought we had was an instruction to attract more of those same things into our life, what would we be inviting in? It would be a great disservice to cheat our future by always nurturing the past, especially the parts that victimize us, even if we truly were victims.

The truth is, I haven't met a person without a painful past. We all have things that can come to haunt us; we all have buttons that will be pushed and unforeseen circumstances that knock us off our feet, and at some point, we will all be dealt a bad hand that leaves us devastated.

Adjusting how you feel about and perceive your life, your own worth, and your ability—and learning to control your emotions—is the only way you will survive. This book will give you that control. Life is not just about surviving—it's about thriving and living days that leave you in wonder. It's about living a wonder-*full* life. You can be so incredibly happy, blissful in mind, radiant in heart, and use that energy to dominate any goal you set.

I know life is also provocative, testing, gruesome, and unforgiving. The privilege of empowerment occurs when you get to know who controls the focus—when you get to know the person behind the lens. The most powerful thing this book does is give you a framework to get to know your Self in a way you probably never have. You are going to take control with mindful observation and constructive perception.

It's the greatest gift, being able to see who you truly are, where you are stuck, and how to happily transform into the version of Self you have always dreamed of becoming.

Energy flows where attention goes.

What you observe, you embody. And what you believe, you attract.

This book will show you exactly how to discover your Self—emotionally, cognitively, and behaviorally. And with the application of some simple neuropsychology, you will be equipped with an intelligent and fruitful understanding of the mind, brain, and body connection that will change the game.

You will learn that if you do not focus on happiness, on the thoughts and emotions that constitute joy, then you risk despair and even depression.

So, the time is now. You are here holding space; congratulate your Self.

It's time to observe life and see wealth, health, beauty, prosperity, love, and abundance. Invite joy every time you see these things, letting them be a reminder of what is possible and what's there for the taking.

I'm ready to get right into making you the happiest you have ever been. Let's get into alignment!

THE AUTHENTICITY GAP OF HAPPINESS

*If you don't know what happiness
really is, you might mistake it
for something else.*

BUT, WHAT EXACTLY
IS HAPPINESS?

I'D LIVED THIRTY YEARS OF MY LIFE HAVING NEVER asked that question.

This question is so critical to our existence that you rarely have an interaction without someone trying to gauge the answer by asking, "How are you?" If you are physically unwell, this is counteracted with concern, empathy, emotional support, and even medical treatment. People often respond supportively when your physical health is compromised, yet your mental health is almost intimidatingly shied away from, or even completely neglected.

Why deny your Self the naked truth of that answer?

Are you *really* happy?

The feeling of happiness is the reason for your life. It is the only measure you should be referencing your Self against.

The goal is joy.

Otherwise, why else are we here?

If you feel resistance to that, take a deep breath, let your guard down, feel your shoulders sink, exhale one long breath, and say to your Self, *the goal of life is joy.*

Inhale now for five seconds.

Hold for five seconds.

Now exhale *slowly* for as long as you can.

Empty your lungs like you have been found after being lost for days at sea.

Now breathe into that relief.

The goal is joy.

So, what makes you feel happy? What is happiness?

At times, the routine that had become my life neglected to integrate such a powerful birthright, my own joy. Instead, I replaced true fulfilment with expectations, obligations, pleasing others, and a multitude of detractors from my happiness. I often said yes to requests, while intrinsically taming the resistance and displeasure of the commitments I made.

Happiness is a completely subjective feeling, an emotional state that is positive. It feels energizing, is pleasant, and is welcomed. It's a feeling of elevation, as the splendor of a high vibrational frequency in your body gets you high.

It's a feeling only you can determine through your Self. You get to decide for your Self what makes you feel like your life is extraordinary, meaningful, and worthwhile.

You are the only determining factor of your measure of happiness.

There have been interesting ways of dictating how to obtain that joy. Sometimes, I have mistakenly put my faith in the material to provide me with such happiness, only to find the feeling to be fleetingly inadequate. The new wardrobe, house, car, and even sometimes the much-looked-forward-to holiday delivered fast-hitting fulfillment, but were unsustainable in their ability to keep the feeling of happiness in perpetuity. I lost interest in chasing materialism, and I did not want to obsess over a better body or gain elite status based on which restaurants I frequented and how often I traveled. Those metrics did little to measure true happiness. I had a good life and I loved my lifestyle, so long as I could afford it. *But,* I wondered, *what would happen to my happiness if I stopped spending?*

Is happiness a financial transaction? Is this how we were designed to experience the best of life? Work to be able to pay for happiness? We use the resources we work so hard to acquire—mostly money, time, and energy—only to watch them deplete, leaving financial burden and a desperate need to get more from the rat race. We then focus on the next hit of happiness in disguise.

But there are alternatives. There are other ways to feel life, to feel happy, to feel fulfilled.

This book is an invitation to explore an alternative approach to life and create sustainable joy.

As I guide you, I welcome your misplaced and silenced curiosity. I open my heart to your discomfort and fury, and I urge you to step forward with bold honesty about your current state of mind. To know that happiness is a feeling means you first have to understand what feelings *are* to understand it.

You feel a lot, every day, all day.

For a person to believe they can escape the emotional intelligence and gravity-defying turbulence of feelings, is to be a corpse dressed in a designer suit.

Feeling escapes no living being.

The investment in getting to know your feelings, your Self, and your happiness is arguably the most important investment you will ever make, with great returns.

So, how are you feeling?

It took me a while to realize that emotions and feelings are different. Feelings are derived from how you perceive your emotions, which are activated in response to a stimulus.

A stimulus is just something that evokes a reaction. We are built to use our senses to process stimuli, and then we generate emotions as a reaction to those stimuli. Most of the time, an emotional reaction is initially instinctive, and you might not give it conscious thought. Or, you might be completely unaware of it. Think of it as your natural autopilot. What you do have control over, however, are the thoughts applied to the emotion, which create your perception and feeling about your world. This is where I felt like I hit the jackpot: when I understood that the thoughts I applied to my emotions created the feelings I had.

Stimulus → Emotion → Applied Thoughts
→ Perception → Feeling

At times I was oblivious or overwhelmed in what I was stimulated by, but now I know our species' reactive mechanism cannot control for stimulus. Sometimes it can't even control for emotion, but we absolutely have control over our feelings.

The buck stops with me, and only me.

I choose the thought around an emotion and how I want to perceive any given situation and its conditions. That is my great power.

It's my ability to choose how to feel about life, and that makes me uniquely individual.

Two people in the exact same circumstances can feel differently. What I am compassionate toward or what I desire comes from what I feel, and that makes me who I am.

We see the world not as it is, but through the lens of our Self.

I had lost hope in humanity when I focused on the wrong things, and I felt despair. My perception of life became completely destructive.

There was darkness there, but there was also light. I let my thinking amplify the wrong emotions instead of diffusing them. I understand my Self, so I know I am an empath. This means that when I walk down Washington Boulevard to Venice Beach in Los Angeles, I notice the homeless and my heart aches for them. I know it's shocking that I walk in LA, but it's shocking to me how many people are numb to the suffering that is streetside every day. Thousands of other people who are on the same street see it painted through the lens of who they are. They see the sign for the yoga studio they joined and never went to, or they might see the sushi place where they celebrated a meaningful anniversary.

Choices.

I have so many choices as to how I perceive the world. I am a collection of preferences that communicate the values I hold deep within my Self.

Perception is a matter of the mind, while emotions are matters of the heart. Nothing hits harder than when your loved ones suffer. Then you help, you learn, you share your hope with each other. I've had an intimate recount of many themes in this book with my best friend, Rose, who shares parts of her story below:

G rowing up was pretty tough for me. I always had a lot to say, and my brain worked faster than the speed of conversations. I often put my foot in my mouth, but I always enjoyed having spirited conversations. The real issue occurred when my mom married her third husband. To be completely honest, she divorced her second husband because he punched me in the face when I was four years old. I had put my middle finger up at the TV. Hopefully now you understand more about how spirited I was. Anyway, my mother married her third husband.

His name was Joe. He was her third cousin, which I thought was truly bizarre, even at nine years old. He didn't have the patience for my wit and sass; he very much wanted me to be a wallflower, and that was never going to happen.

After just a mere three months, Joe turned from "prince charming" to every woman's nightmare, and my mother had a mental breakdown. I remember waking up from my sleep one night to find my mother about to stab herself in the stomach because "Joey boy" accused her of cheating and was threatening her life. I begged her to stop and asked her to think of my sister and me. Luckily, she listened.

After that episode, there were many more. During one in particular, I was standing next to Joe, and I don't remember specifically what I said, but he took his elbow and jabbed me in the face. I remember it hurting a lot, but all I could focus on was telling my dad. I knew Charlie would sort everything out. I called my dad that evening to tell him everything that had happened over the past few months. I needed to leave my mother's house and go live with him in Antigua. My dad was a pilot, and as you could imagine, looking after a preteen by himself wouldn't be feasible. However, Charlie managed to wrangle something, and within three weeks my parents signed a contract and I boarded a Twin Otter Dash 8 to Antigua.

The relief I felt was insane, and that's when I felt like life really began for me.

Finally, I had a parent who put me first. I never looked back. Three months later, my mother's husband pulled the trigger of a gun, and the bullet grazed my mom's temple. She moved out that evening. I sometimes wonder if it would have been me, had I stayed.

I think because I was exposed to adult problems at a very young age, such as drug use, suicide, and alcohol abuse, it made me incredibly grateful to create a new life. I built a foundation purposefully based on love, happiness, contentment, and other core values. I believe those fundamentals created a happy and content life for my husband, my dog Winston, and myself.

Overall, mindset and perception are everything, I was super young and naive in many ways while in a dangerous situation, but I was always incredibly positive and focused on finding a solution. I believe that mindset helped me find a way out, and luckily I had a parent who had my best interests at heart.

Sharing stories like these takes guts, vulnerability, and the purging of a lot of fear. There is so much to unpack emotionally with hidden traumas you experience and how you perceive them. If we never talk about them and never seek to understand them, they will set us back for many lives to come, as you will learn in the coming chapters.

THE PERCEPTION PHENOMENON

Change the way you look at things and
the things you look at change.

—Wayne Dyer

Perception pairs stimulation with existing knowledge and experience to find understanding and meaning. You can perceive consciously or without conscious awareness. I learned to interpret my life by asking how meaningful or meaningless my various experiences were.

How do I perceive my choices and what feelings do I experience?

My beliefs and values are prejudices that influence my judgment and perception of all things. Some beliefs and values I feel from my core and ignite me naturally; some are simply learned and adopted because they're the norm, or because that's the way it's always been. Some are part of the conditioning and culture I was exposed to.

Do my values really matter to me, or do they matter because I was told they were supposed to matter? Do I feel my values are authentically important, and can I see how they influence my happiness? For instance, if I value integrity, innovation, or philanthropy, then these ideals drive my behavior and expectations of Self. My motivation, how I prioritize choices, try new things, and uphold my honor dictate how I behave. Essentially, I choose my actions to align with my expectations, as they are critically underpinned by my values.

By the title of this book, I am sure you can tell authenticity and happiness are a large part of my core values, but for a long time I didn't even know what my top three values were. I took a few assessments, like the free resources online by the Barrett Values Centre, and those started me on the journey to choose from a variety of words that came to be my value concepts. You always start somewhere if you are evolving. You are not born an expert, and even when you reach the epitome of your field, the field itself might change.

You should value progression, Self-evolution, and the journey as it unfolds in the daily experience of life.

It's never too late to approach this with some curiosity and explore that part of your Self. It sure does make life a whole lot clearer when you know what's important to you, and when you know what happiness feels like.

My expectations, opinions, the focus of my attention, my memory, and my existing knowledge base all shape my perception. Learned thinking patterns are paired with emerging emotions to create the feelings I have about my life. To put my feelings at the forefront of experience is to know I can measure my alignment with my expectations, and when they match up, that's where I find bliss. I live for that state of life fulfillment.

Expectations ← vs. → Experience

I've experienced so many feelings, from sadness to happiness, hate to love, fear to courage, and I've bravely taken the journey to discover the root of my emotions. I've found that the contrast between my experience and the expectation I had influenced my feelings. For instance, in a job interview I expect to be the one on trial. I expect that the interviewer holds the cards and I have to impress them. Most of us believe we can get the jobs we interview for, otherwise we wouldn't apply, but our little expectations give power to the assessment and validation of the HR department. For example, I look at their expressions to decide how I feel about the experience. If I expect them to be responsive and positive and hint that I'd be a fit for the company, but they do no such thing, I may completely misread my experience.

My expectations influence how I perceive my experience.

Without holding firm to my expectations and objectively perceiving my experience instead, it allows me to analyze a spectrum of potentials as to how the interview actually went.

Am I proud? Am I learning where I can improve my communication skills? Did I identify some of my weaknesses during the interview? And most importantly, did I even ask my Self if I like *them*? Is this company a good fit for me? There were times when I felt angry about a situation, but by simply choosing to think of it as a growth opportunity, it changed the anger immediately. I thought, *Hey, I got into the room, gained more experience as an interviewee, and was exposed to different hiring tactics. This means I have evolved in knowledge and experience.* My mindset and perception are choices, and sometimes positives appear when, initially, I didn't feel like there were any.

If anger is not managed with the right mindset, I can perceive a bad outcome as a reflection of my Self, and not just the situation. I have done it before—embodied what happened as failure, taken it personally, and let it cut deep until it eventually led me to think, *I am a failure.* When really, I failed at *one interview.* If you question your Self-worth long enough, you trickle into a feeling of shame from rejection, and before you know it, you are in a spiral of despair.

Perception and perspective go hand in hand. I perceive a situation, I feel it, and I can even be positive about it when it's isolated, but in the context of the whole, I can find supporting evidence to strengthen my perception. Perspective can be destructive if I choose to look at everyone who has a job and say, "Look how many people can get employment. Look at how many people have their dream jobs, yet I can't even get a callback." Or, I can look at how many people have persevered and gotten jobs and have done what I am trying to do. My dream job is worth fighting for, and I'm sure lots of others had to exercise resilience and perseverance to get where they are.

The same things can look different based on how you perceive them and the perspective you place them in. As illustrated by the Müller-Lyer illusion below, do the black lines appear to be different lengths to you?

The following Müller-Lyer illusion features lines that appear to be different lengths when they are in fact identical.

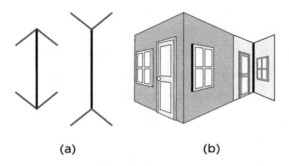

(a)   (b)

Diagram 1.1: In the Müller-Lyer illusion, lines appear to be different lengths, although they are identical. (a) Arrows at the ends of lines may make the line on the right appear longer, although the lines are the same length. (b) When applied to a three-dimensional image, the line on the right again may appear longer, although both black lines are the same length.

Lumen Learning (2020). *Introduction to Psychology*. Retrieved from https://courses.lumen learning.com/msstate-waymaker-psychology/chapter/reading-what-is-perception.

You will have a different mindset and feeling depending upon your perception and perspective.

To feel and control feeling is to decide your happiness.

As humans we almost always perceive from a point of stimulus. This is automated and sometimes doesn't even register in our consciousness. Instinctive perception is our immediate reaction, which assumes that a situation is a certain way. Mindful perception allows us to consider perspectives and respond from clear consciousness. Attention without judgment has helped me practice mindful perception. The importance of nonjudgment allows me to observe situations without embodying destructive or irrational emotions, as I hold space from what is happening and how I allow it to impact me. With this objective and mindful observation, I can perceive things in ways that leave me feeling happier.

Perceptual expectancy imposes a set of expectations and creates a predisposition to perception. I expect things to be a certain way, so I perceive situations to affirm my expectations. I am constantly seeing the world as I am, not how it actually is. This makes me uniquely human and individual. Two people in the same situation can perceive it very differently. The difference in our preferences and desires include tastes, cuisines, sports, fashion, music, partners, jobs, and the list goes on. It's rational that our perception of life itself and our happiness will be based on how we define our preferences and includes our expectation of how such feelings can be procured. You also may experience sensory adaptation, where you grow accustomed to how an environment or experience stimulates you. There are times when I become numb to the endless sources of happiness that are all around me, waiting for my perceptual experience and awareness so they can be felt and enjoyed.

Perceptual Expectancy vs. Perceptual Experience

Perception is my ability to engage my mind with an awareness of stimuli and process it through my senses. I perceive both subconsciously and consciously. The perceptual experience will be largely influenced by my desire to justify my beliefs and reaffirm them. My perceptual expectancy influences the way I experience the world, purely based on what I expect. When my expectations and experiences do not match up, I find myself affected by an Authenticity Gap of Happiness.

THE AUTHENTICITY GAP
OF HAPPINESS

How often do you ask your Self, "How do I feel about this, and can I clearly identify the emotion I am feeling?" Your feelings shape your expectations, so Self-awareness of your emotions also impacts your experience. Expectation and beliefs go hand in hand, because past experiences contribute to why you believe the things you do. For example, our expectation of danger drives fear. Your expectation of recognition is sometimes the seed from which rejection is planted, because without seeking validation you would not perceive an absence of it, making you feel rejected. It is therefore critical to understand what and who influences your beliefs and your expectations of the world, and even more so, of your Self.

When I started to take ownership of my expectations or the ways in which my life experience fell short of what I hoped for, that's when I started to understand the concept of Authenticity. In some cases, I used justification to defend the gap between my expectations and experience, but were they really rooted in truth? Or were they rooted in excuses? Was it possible my expectations left too much room for disappointing experiences? Was it possible I failed to put effort into my experiences to meet my expectations? I'm sure we've all done it: adjusted the goal and what we expect of our Selves in the face of diminishing effort, so we don't have to feel the discomfort of this gap.

When there is too much discord between what you expect and what you experience, you create what I call an Authenticity Gap of Happiness. This gap is where disappointment, discouragement, despair, and eventually depression exist. This gap was my breeding ground for suicidal thinking.

The Authenticity Gap is a methodology studied by Fleishman-Hillard to help companies understand and proactively manage the gap between audiences' expectations and actual experiences with a company or brand. It examines whether or not products or services meet the expectations of a customer, essentially looking at customer satisfaction.

I applied this methodology to explore the Authenticity Gap of Happiness for life satisfaction as it relates to short- and long-term happiness, and pleasure in instant and delayed gratifications.

I decided this gap would focus on the difference between expectations [beliefs] and experience [behavior] as measured by the thoughts and emotions that make up the psychological state. It's through our feelings that we can monitor our fulfillment of life, the perception of desire, and our level of satisfaction.

I wondered what the Authenticity Gap of Happiness felt like for others, so I asked my friend Pete, who for a majority of our relationship I referred to as "the juice guy." The first time we met, we had green juice, and since then I've watched him live what I would call a ravishingly epic life filled with happiness. He seemed to have a grip on fulfillment across the board, professionally and personally. Pete's career path included over fifteen years in the financial services industry. Goldman Sachs approached him for a graduate role when he was still an undergraduate student. He seized the opportunity, which led to an accelerated induction into the industry with a double bachelor degree in commerce and finance. Pete went on to work with some of the world's best finance and investment companies, such as Macquarie Private Bank and National Australia Bank (NAB). His adventure continues with the entrepreneurial venture and PropTech startup Trulet, whose purpose is to reimagine the global property rental landscape through artificial intelligence and machine learning.

So, what did Pete have to say when I dropped the concept of the Authenticity Gap of Happiness?

Fascinating! In private banking we talk about
"closing the gap" of perception and reality. This is because
of something called cognitive dissonance, which is a
state of mental conflict as a result of the choices presented
to you. I think it's much harder to overcome an
Authenticity Gap of Happiness, because at the end of the
day this is as vulnerable as you can get with yourself.
I guess for me, I surround myself with those
that can measure it (in me) themselves.
The key is to talk about it openly with those you trust.
They care and won't judge you if you're not happy.

First, let's decipher what cognitive dissonance is, so we can better understand the conflict it can cause. In psychology, it's recognized as the inconsistency among one's thoughts, beliefs, and attitudes, especially relating to behavior and decisions. If you hold contradictory beliefs or values, or take an action that goes against your beliefs and values, then you experience stress as a response. As Pete states, it requires a level of vulnerability to speak of that mental conflict and the Authenticity Gap of Happiness that occurs as a result, but as Aristotle once said, "Knowing yourself is the beginning of all wisdom."

WHAT MAKES ME MY SELF?

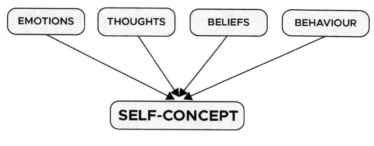

Diagram 1.2

Your emotions, thoughts, beliefs, and behavior are what make you your Self.

Your feelings are driven by the emotions and thoughts you have when you perceive them. Your beliefs dictate what you hold to be true and are a product of your memories and opinions. They form your understanding of the world and your expectations while living in it. Your behavior is how you obtain knowledge through action, and this shapes your experience.

It's important to understand that new behaviors can lead to new experiences and new ways of thinking, and thereby, new beliefs. When my beliefs change, it drives new choices in my behavior. The relationships between these four dimensions of Self are so multi-layered in cause and effect that there are a variety of feedback loops. You can change your thoughts around certain emotions that allow you to be either reactive or responsive. Changing your thoughts and emotions changes your perception, which in turn influences your choices, attitudes, and behavior.

You should think about how you are activated by your emotions, thoughts, beliefs, and behavior, and the impact each has on your level of happiness. Do you resolve conflict easily, or do you hold on to anger and resentment? Is that because you are unwilling to let go of the beliefs that justify those emotions? This sometimes happens in relationships when one person has trust issues: based on their beliefs, they make assumptions regarding the behavior and level of honesty of the other person. It creates a discord in the relationship as the person who cannot trust believes it's not safe to do so, and the person that cannot gain the trust feels unsettled, knowing their partner does not trust them.

The relationship between beliefs and behavior, and similarly your emotions and thoughts and all the ways the four of them intertwine, is complex to say the least, but it's also riveting.

To be happy, you need to get to know each of these Self activators:

Emotions. I like to think of these as instinctive or intuitive states that are distinguishable from reason or knowledge. They arise naturally from nonconscious effort, sort of like subconscious messages. The degree of pleasure or displeasure I experience creates a spectrum of emotions and varying biological states, as my emotions and biology are linked, not just my psychology.

Thoughts. These include anything that comes to mind like concepts, ideas, and opinions, that are generated through experiencing my life. Thoughts can be aim-oriented to help me evaluate and make conclusions, they can serve as processing tools to register my experiences, or they can be analytical. The organization of my thoughts forms my intellectual capability.

Beliefs. Acceptance that a statement is true and an attitude of confidence, trust, and faith in the validity of ideas and concepts makes up your beliefs. It doesn't matter if these beliefs are true or false—the fact that you believe them to be true does.

Behavior. This is the way I act, react, and interact with others and my environment. It's a means to express my feelings, needs, and thoughts.

Your expectations are shaped by what you believe you deserve, and they create your desires. Your experiences, however, are shaped by your choice of actions, creating your level of satisfaction. If you take action and then evaluate how you feel about the action, this gives insight as to whether you should *approach or avoid* the same behaviors in the future. You learn what you like by trying different things. This starts to reveal just how important the "action" part of your life can be, rather than just the thinking parts. Action taken in relation to an expectation can result in many emotions, such as disappointment, overwhelm, encouragement, and pride.

Your intention and mindset preceding and subsequent to the action are also important.

Thinking you should do something, believing it is a good thing, and then actually following through with the behavior creates alignment, leaving you in a happy emotional state. This alignment closes the gap between expectation and experience and keeps you happy.

If the concept of being happy was as simple as the five letters that construct the word, we would all easily be in a state of joy. "Happy," however, is deceivingly complex.

HEDONIC HAPPINESS
VS. EUDAIMONIC HAPPINESS

Happiness is subjective and constitutes positive feelings around the ways in which you are satisfied with your life. The phenomenon of happiness was originally explored back in the fourth century BC, when

Greek philosophy was all the rave. There was a philosopher, Aristippus, who deemed that life should be focused primarily on maximizing pleasure, and this was when the concept of hedonic happiness took shape. When the light of psychology was shed onto the philosophy of hedonic happiness, it revealed that perspective was a key part of determining the psychological and physiological pleasures of both the mind and the body. As a human species, we are pleasure-seeking, but we will always place avoidance of pain over obtaining pleasure. Maximizing hedonic happiness became about increasing pleasure and decreasing pain.

This is why survival will always precede satisfaction, as demonstrated by the famous pyramid created by Abraham Maslow, which shows the hierarchy of human of needs. If I'm about to be eaten by a bear, I'm sure I can put a pause on consuming those delicious s'mores. After all, if I'm dead, it doesn't matter what may have brought me pleasure. We are, at our most primal level, conditioned to first and foremost avoid pain. As we grew accustomed to avoiding pain and surviving, we may have become victims of our own evolutionary conditioning, rather than progressing beyond basic needs toward Self-actualization and reaching our greatest potential.

Self-actualization is the quintessential pinnacle of our happy existence, when we capitalize on our intrinsic psychology to grow, and we use our skills to their maximum capacity and realize our full potential. To look beyond immediate pleasure and basic Self-survival means you look beyond instant gratification and pleasure and find joy in flourishing. This style of happiness became known as eudaimonic happiness.

As the concept of happiness evolved, Aristotle proposed the eudaimonic happiness phenomenon, which is to live a life in accordance with virtues. The word eudaimonia stems from the Greek words eu (good) and daimon (spirit), so acting in accordance with such "good spirit" is to live a life of virtue. Embracing the characteristics of virtue would result in the attainment of moral excellence, and this was thought to be another realm of happiness. This is the kind that I personally strive toward. Virtuous beings are often admired for their attitudes and have successfully satisfied their love, connection, and Self-esteem needs.

In contrast with hedonic happiness and the pursuit of momentary pleasure, which focuses on instant gratification, eudaimonic happiness is the pursuit of purpose, and the impact of gratification is delayed. I have found a combination of both to be the winning approach to being holistically happy. Take my word for it: instant pleasure alone doesn't leave you feeling happy as years pass and you tally up the scoreboard.

The reason authentic happiness requires a blend of the two is that you adapt to your happiness, so if you focus solely on hedonic happiness and hit your pleasure points of success, experiences, lifestyle, etc., you will revert to a baseline set point of happiness as the novelty of instant gratification fades. And fade, it shall. If your set point is vibrationally low and you are hiding authentic emotions of sadness, despair, or dissatisfaction, then that is where you will return when the feelings of hedonic happiness subside. This is known as the "hedonic treadmill." It's the tendency to pursue pleasure after pleasure to keep reigniting emotions of joy that will naturally wear off.

Hedonic adaptation also applies to destructive emotions, as they too shall pass and fade, thank goodness. The severity of suffering adapts in the same manner as happiness. The automatic intelligence of the body will honor its one dominant goal: returning to its preferred balanced state of homeostasis. This adaptation works with your biological systems, as well as your psychological and spiritual systems, to always bring you back to center.

The Hedonic Treadmill

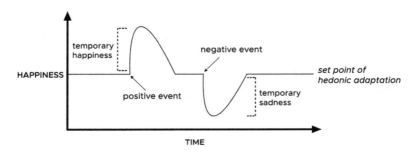

Diagram 1.3

Hedonic adaptation is the return to neutrality and emotional equilibrium after a short time. Subsequent to an event, regardless if the experience was positive or negative, you will inevitably return to your set point of happiness, or default state of existence. The ecstasy of new love sees the end of its honeymoon period, the unbearable nature of grief finds a new home in nostalgic laughter, and all in all, you return to where you started. A study by Harvard psychologist Daniel Gilbert featured in his 2004 TED Talk became what he calls "the poster study" for hedonic adaptation. In a nutshell, he found that lottery winners returned to their prewinning state of financial satisfaction a year later, when they were expected to be happier. Paraplegics, just twelve months after losing the use of their legs, were not as unhappy as people would have assumed them to be. Many superior studies have since more conclusively proven the power of hedonic adaptation.

The Intelligence of Happiness

So where exactly is that state of equilibrium? What's the set point you return to?

Heritage of Our Happiness

I never really thought genetics created a predisposition to our set point of happiness and that our current state of circumstances would be influenced by cellular biological fabric. You kind of think about genetics as hair color, eye color, height, or even the probability of inheriting illnesses, but happiness was not something I categorized as a DNA hand-me-down. To me, happiness had to do with feeling, perception, perspective, and the emotional intelligence to choose your state of being. The plot twist is that DNA, personality, and happiness all are part of your biological heritage. Amit Etkin from the Department of Psychiatry and Behavioral Sciences at Stanford School of Medicine has studied the genetics of happiness and believes there is correlation between genetics and positive emotion. In addition, Meike Bartels, University Research Professor in Genetics and Well-being at the Department of Biological Psychology at Vrije Universiteit Amsterdam, which maintains the Netherlands Twin Register, has also explored whether genes or environment determine happiness.

I was fascinated to learn that up to 50 percent of your set point of happiness is attributed to genetics, with external factors affecting just a mere 10 percent. The magic 40 percent is within your control: it's the subjectivity of your happiness and your choice to feel it, or at least, that's what the research says.

I know how powerful our genes are, but I believe that faith is bigger than assuming one's fate.

I believe you can take more control of your happiness by desensitizing negativity and replacing it with positive reinforcement. You know which thoughts feel negative because they create a disruptive stress in the body; it's anything but calming. You can eradicate pessimism and happiness inhibitors by practicing optimism. Ask your Self, *does it feel good to think about this? Can I look at this in a positive light?* I could have been upset about the statistics, and I could have felt like I didn't have control. I hoped the science would say I control my happiness and that would be the silver lining. Sometimes you have to create your silver lining, and that, for me, was believing in something positive and thinking, *Yes, I can. I can control my happiness completely!*

There is one catch, though. First, I have to know who I am before I can find out what makes me happy.

SELF-CONCEPT
& LIFE
SATISFACTION

―――――

If you do not know your Self,
how will you know what
makes you happy?

T HIS PERCEPTION THAT I ALLOW TO RECKLESSLY cradle me while I lay on the clay-tiled floor of my studio apartment is glorifiably victimizing and utterly irrational. I let the way I perceive my life, my worth, my Self as a human be painted with pessimism and brushed over with a gloss of disgust. I can't find a way to love who I am, and I start to think, who am I actually?

If I can't figure out who I am, how could I possibly be happy with my Self?

I am a strategist. I outline meticulous plans. I cross-reference my time versus energy investments against my intentions of impact. I manage my objectives well, I show up, I deliver. If I've done this so admirably, how am I not at all satisfied with my life? The cold tiles invite the faintest goosebumps to crawl on my skin. I feel the tension of my collarbones and shoulders weighed down by my scrutinizing lack of clarity.

Am I on the right track in life? Did I make all the wrong turns? What am I even living for?

I realize it's not just happiness that matters at this moment; I need to have hope in where I am going.

Where is life taking me?

I question my very own existence and why it matters.

I have no answers, and at this moment I really don't know who I am. I do not know why I am here. I realize that reclaiming my purpose is the only lifeline to pull me out of decaying while in the fetal position and being swallowed alive by a heartless existence.

To be happy, my life needs to mean something.

I want it to be meaning*full*, not meaningless.

HAPPINESS VS.
LIFE SATISFACTION

I have learned the critical difference between happiness and life satisfaction.

A eudaimonic approach to happiness puts purpose and meaning as greater priorities. Happiness itself is an emotion you feel in the moment; it is immediate in its experiential capacity and generally quite fleeting. Happiness in solitude, however, won't lead to a fulfilled life. It's a part of life satisfaction, but not the only construct of it.

Building on the work of Daniel Gilbert, professor of psychology at Harvard University, the meaning of happiness is captured as "anything we pleased" in a transitory state. Happiness is influenced by varying experiences, and I have found it can be achieved through mindset, optimism, and positive thinking. Life satisfaction is much more long-lived, as you maintain a stable feeling about your whole life with past, present, and future considered. I can feel happy about a moment, but that's limited to my individual feeling, while life satisfaction is often a feeling that summarizes the consolidation of my friend and family relationships, work, finances, health, wellness, and personal development.

The Gallup World Poll releases a World Happiness Report based on surveys taken in more than 160 countries in more than 140 languages, and uses the Cantril ladder (Cantril, 1965), also known as the self-anchoring scale, to gauge happiness and satisfaction in life. Albert Hadley Cantril Jr. was a Princeton University psychologist who invented the Cantril ladder as a methodology in the life evaluation poll. It prompts respondents to answer the following question:

*Please imagine a ladder, with steps
numbered from 0 at the bottom to 10 at the top.
The top of the ladder represents the best possible life
for you and the bottom of the ladder represents
the worst possible life for you. On which step of
the ladder would you say you personally
feel you stand at this time?*

Values in the map range from zero (the worst possible life they can imagine) to ten (the best possible life they could imagine), represented as different steps on the ladder. Based on the responses, individuals are categorized as suffering, struggling, or thriving.

Now for the shocker.

In 2020, the stats on people thriving have dropped a staggering 46.4 percent, which matches the low point of the 2008 Great Recession. These figures were the lowest levels in the thirteen-year history of Gallup's reporting. Many more people are struggling or suffering than you might assume. If you are one of those people, know that you are not alone, and there is a roadmap on how to live a thriving life right here in this book.

For a number of years, the only country to rank above eight was Finland, which in 2020 was ranked as the happiest country with a score of 7.769. Perhaps it's because of their stoicism and impassiveness to the seesaw of pain and pleasure that is life. Or, it could be their notable grit and the positive perseverance, resilience, and more eudaimonic long-term approach to happiness. Regardless, they are the exception to the majority. And while sevens are happy, they aren't *super* happy.

I'm not one to settle for averagely happy when I could be amazingly happy.

For a time, I considered happiness and success to be the same thing, and that was my first mistake.

While success in business is largely measured by customer satisfaction, I think you can measure happiness by life satisfaction. The Satisfaction with Life Scale (SWLS) is a single scale used by UNESCO, the CIA, the New Economics Foundation, the World Health Organization, and the United Nations to measure how one views their Self-esteem, well-being, and overall happiness with life. At the core of life satisfaction are emotions and feelings about your life's direction and the options available for your future. Front and center in focus is the Self, or the concept of Self, and the perception of one's ability to cope with daily life.

LIFE SATISFACTION AND SELF-CONCEPT

If you do not know your Self, you really won't know what makes you happy as an individual.

So, before you end up on the floor of your home wondering who the hell's life you are living and not recognizing what makes you thrive, take a moment to breathe.

Discovering what makes you your Self is a process, not a one-day event. If you think you already know who you are, then fantastic, you are one of few. Only 10–15 percent of people are Self-aware, and to possess that unique quality is to have an advantage in your Self intelligence. Also, most of the 10–15 percent do not actually believe they are Self-aware. The work begins with the awareness of what makes you who you are.

If you are in the 85–90 percent who need to develop Self-awareness, then you are already ahead by choosing to read this book and invest in your Self-discovery. Self-awareness is one of the healthiest traits you can develop, and is critical to helping you close your Authenticity Gap of Happiness. How can you meet your expectations of life without first being aware of what they are? Your beliefs, values, and internal Self-talk create the foundation of expectation, your personality, and the ways in which you behave.

The goal is to use Self-awareness to align your ideal Self and beliefs with your actual Self and behaviors.

$$\text{Expectations} \leftarrow \text{vs.} \rightarrow \text{Experience}$$
$$\text{Beliefs} \leftarrow \text{vs.} \rightarrow \text{Behaviors}$$
$$\text{Ideals} \leftarrow \text{vs.} \rightarrow \text{Actuality}$$

The concept of Self-awareness was first defined in 1972 by T. Shelley Duval and Robert Wicklund as a focused attention on our Selves that evaluates and compares current behavior to internal standards and values. This drives an objective Self-consciousness. Learning how to be objective about my Self empowered me to be accountable, and it made me welcome constructive criticism much more because I was already summing up my Self on my own.

When you can clearly and objectively identify your beliefs, then you can understand your motivations, monitor your thoughts and emotions, and create perceptions that leave you in a positive state of joy. You do this by asking yourself *why*? Why do you have that opinion? Why do you have the expectations you have? Why do you predict certain outcomes?

"Why" is your friend. Ask why, and see what thoughts start circulating.

Without this kind of reflection, you might be mismanaging stress, pain, past trauma, and living by limiting or false beliefs. Your long-term Life Satisfaction can be compromised if you aren't aware of the ways you stay out of alignment with your dimensions of Self: your emotions, thoughts, beliefs, and behavior. Through introspection of ideals contrasted with reflection on your reality in actualizing them, you can start to identify how to close the gap and experience greater levels of happiness.

Mindfulness, like Self-awareness, has helped me consciously monitor and filter thoughts, but it also allows me to be present and aware of my emotions as they fluctuate and change. Different experiences breed different feelings. My identity and the perception of being uniquely individual has much to do with my Self-awareness as I decipher my personality and the behaviors that make me who I am. Asking why I do what I do helps me get clear on my motivations—it helps me uncover purpose.

Self-conscious is actually one of my favorite things to be, nurturing the preoccupation with my Self and realizing I exist in this world as a body, experiencing life in varying environments. I then start to see how I interact, reason, and create scenarios to pursue my desires and obtain satisfaction.

The philosophy of Self will examine consciousness as an awareness of one's internal and external existence in relation to their beliefs and values. It also considers the agency of your ability to take action. Can you do what you think about doing? The psychology of Self, on the other hand, looks at your mind and behavior as it relates to your Self-esteem, Self-knowledge, and Self-efficacy. These are the dimensions that I believe make up Self-concept. They are all integral parts to close the Authenticity Gap of Happiness, as each dimension hinges on how you curate beliefs and expectations of your Self.

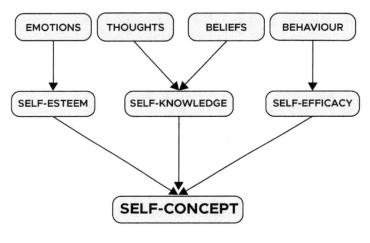

Diagram 2.1

When I lacked this sense of Self, I experienced a stagnation loop where I kept feeling like I wanted to progress but never actually made any progress. My expectations of my Self were not being met by my experience of Self, and the emotions that resulted from that were destructive. One of the greatest contributors to psychology in the twentieth century, Carl Rogers, had a humanist mindset and believed people are driven by the basic motive to fulfill their potential to the highest capacity. I feel him on that one, and I think this notion resembles that of the Self-actualization peak of Maslow's Hierarchy of Needs pyramid. It's natural that we strive to reach our greatest potential as a part of being human, and Rogers believed that individuals become destructive when they embody a poor Self-concept or when the process of actualizing their value is compromised.

I'm sure you have felt inspired to do more with your life, to live differently, or to pursue new goals that require change. Perhaps you have the desire to get healthier, find a partner, be a better parent, gain more recognition at work, or even jump into the world of entrepreneurship. It's more than likely you aren't completely happy with life as you are living it, and there's a desire for change, improvement, and a pursuit of greater well-being. This is where you can see the hedonic adaptation taking place: you have become less indulged by your routine life, and that quick hit of happiness and instant pleasure in the moment has faded in comparison to the fire burning for more meaning and true happiness.

I've had thoughts and ideas that have gotten me excited, and I've made plans to execute such ideas, but the truth is, between the idea and the realization of it, something happens. Inspiration fades, and action is left untaken. I'd find myself stagnating back to my set point, but it was always worse because I'd have more regrets about the things I did not achieve. I'd feel disappointment, guilt, shame, and utter sadness.

Clearly defining my sense of Self has helped me develop a positive mindset, affirmative thinking, Self-enhancing beliefs, and the agency we spoke about earlier that drives behaviors. These factors can help you accomplish goals and find your joy. You are inherently driven by the motivation to Self-actualize, which means if you do not know your Self, you may never get clear on what you want. Without truly knowing what you want, I fear you will just end up struggling to decide on a destination, and that stagnation loop will inch you into avoidable suffering.

I am adamant that a lack of Self-clarity makes a person unsure of who they are at their core. Without Self-clarity, it's common to change your mind often and to have doubts and fears kill your dreams as you stagnate in a rabbit hole, unsure of how to get out of the choices you committed to.

I know my Self-clarity is what was compromised when I wrote my suicide letter. I lost my sense of Self and my perception of worthiness (esteem). I had given up on my own ability to be great (efficacy), and I hated that I hadn't accomplished what I wanted in life yet. My Self-image was distorted, my emotions were out of control, and for a long time I did not take that seriously.

Happiness and your right to fight for it are valid. If you hate where you are right now, that's real.

If you do not address your Self-concept, one day you might end up on the wrong side of depression. So please love your Self enough to put your Self first.

As mentioned in the Gallup studies, most people are either suffering or struggling, and a mere handful are actually thriving. Those who make it out of suffering and into struggle are to be commended, but you don't want to just labor through life. You want to thrive. And that helping hand to obtain a thriving life starts with understanding who you are.

The goal is to find alignment between what you expect of your Self and how you believe you can accomplish it. This will help you identify and close your Authenticity Gap of Happiness.

Your desires will be met with satisfaction.

SELF-ALIGNMENT

I define alignment as when you feel your life experience matches your expectations, because what you think, believe, and do leave you in a positive mental and emotional state. You perceive life as joyous, hopeful, and rewarding. Self-Alignment will be what determines your well-being in emotional, mental, physical, spiritual, social, and environmental capacities.

THE THREE SELVES

> *Knowing others is wisdom. Knowing the self*
> *is enlightenment. Mastering others requires*
> *force. Mastering the self requires strength.*
>
> —Lao Tzu, *Tao Te Ching* (1972)

You often hear people saying, "I am who I am," or before auditions or interviews, they'll say, "Just be yourself." But how can you fully understand your Self and how can you make your Self happy? The intimidating nature of life in its entirety is overwhelming; there are so many moving parts among who you are in your career, your relationships, your wellness, your community, and the list goes on. To know your Self right now is to know your Self entirely.

The Self is an individual person as the object of its own reflective consciousness.

While Self-image looks at how you view your Self, my model of Self-concept also includes what you think and feel about your Self.

It encourages you to use your Self-awareness to observe and reflect upon the dimensions of alignment among emotions, thoughts, beliefs, and behavior.

These dimensions are pivotal, and I have summed them up into three Selves that make up your Self-concept, which are the following:

- **The Affective Self,** or felt Self, which centralizes emotions and Self-esteem that landscape our beliefs, values, and the subjective way we measure our own worth. In psychology, to explore Affect is to look at the underlying feelings, emotions, and moods that create one's experience. The Affective Self will highlight the emotions that help monitor Self-esteem, such as shame or pride, courage, regret, guilt, and even rejection, despair, or depression around our value.

- **The Cognitive Self,** or known Self, focuses on the thoughts and beliefs that shape our Self-knowledge. This Cognitive Self is determined by what we think we're like as a person—it's our Self-awareness and the Self-consciousness that determine our personality and individuality. Self-knowledge is constructed as we adopt existing beliefs, form new beliefs from world experiences, and internalize information as truth. All knowledge is not created equal. The ways in which we process information, give it meaning, and hold it to be true will change our Cognitive Self-concept.

- **The Executive Self,** agent or active Self, tunes into our behaviors and Self-efficacy. This version of Self highlights our belief in our ability to behave in ways that achieve desired performance. It looks at Self-confidence and motivation.

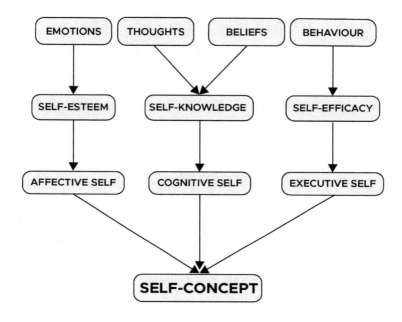

Diagram 2.2

One's Self-concept revolves around different beliefs in their Self-image, ability, and worldview. This all impacts how we take action, and getting to know our Executive Self aids in enhancing our behavioral psychology and executing behaviors to close the gap.

THE AFFECTIVE 'FELT' SELF
& SELF-ESTEEM

---

*Gallup's Global Emotions Report tracks a fundamental
element of the human experience:* emotion.
*Globally, how people feel is a powerful force.
It can forge the destiny of a nation or
just the shape of a day.*

—Gallup 2020 Global Emotions Report

Our feelings are valid. They are powerful individually and collectively. To understand the emotional component of feeling, you need to consider the state of your Affective "felt" Self.

The Affective Self, at its most primal level, is the way you feel a stimulus or experience instinctively from a non-conscious place, usually driven by your survival instinct and reptilian brain. You respond to a stimulus that is experienced through your emotions.

Three men's pooled knowledge of neuroscience and neuroanatomy contributed to the understanding of the interconnectedness of brain structures and our emotional experience. This brought about the term limbic system. The brain's limbic system—or if you like big words, the paleomammalian cortex—directly relates to our instantaneous emotional response and the affective system that curates our judgments and discernment. It's like the control center for our reactions.

Self-awareness in regards to our Affective Self will help correlate our emotions to our motivation and behavior.

Our brains have three sections to consider:

- The *emotional brain or limbic system*, which is located in the amygdala and relates to pain and pleasure. This is the processing center for stimuli.
- The *reptilian survival brain* deals with the fight, flight, freeze, or stress response and pain avoidance. This part of the brain focuses on safety.
- The *thinking brain or neocortex* is the reasoning brain, which is pleasure-seeking. This part of the brain focuses on satisfaction.

The three brains integrate emotions and thoughts that generate biochemical interactions, influencing our feelings and state of happiness. We literally produce chemical neurotransmitters that allow us to feel pleasure or suppress pain, based on how our brain engages the Affective Self. As you experience emotions, the brain then instructs you to react with instinct or reason, but it will always place your safety needs (pain avoidance) as priority over your satisfaction needs (pleasure-seeking). The survival brain will always override the thinking brain if the emotions of fear, anger, anxiety, disgust, etc. are present. Your survival mode and the instinct to protect your Self serves to avoid danger or pain, even in the form of negative emotions. Emotions activate your fight, flight, or freeze response. This stress response is an emergency state meant only to be activated when there is a threat to life, and it's intended to be short-lasting. This was one of the most important things I learned.

One of the most crucial biological systems in your body is the endocrine system, which is made up of glands that produce chemical substances known as hormones. During fight or flight, your endocrine system will release hormones, such as cortisol, that enhance your ability to survive under threatening circumstances. The required behavior—in this circumstance, for instance, actually fighting or fleeing—uses the hormones as a resource to perform required acts for survival.

This is your body's way of making sure you have the energy to perform any action required to live. It assumes you will use the energy and after it's used, the body will return to balance, or homeostasis, just like you return to a set point of happiness and emotional equilibrium.

The body always wants to return to balance.

You can only address life satisfaction when you keep your Self alive, and according to your brain, if your mind is stressed, you are under a death threat. This is such a critical point of understanding, because if you cannot control your emotions, you cannot move from survival into greater states of happiness and long-term life satisfaction. This is the difference between living in suffering, struggling, and thriving. Be aware of your Affective Self and aim to control your emotions. Become master of your mind and navigator of your brain. We will learn a few techniques in Chapters 4 and 5 that show you how to do just that.

For now, it might be helpful to clarify that your brain and its neu-rological functions deal with your biology and its systems, like the endocrine and nervous systems, while your mind looks at psycholog-ical elements, such as your emotions and your thoughts.

I reached a turning point in my happiness when I started to ask if I was burying my emotions—if I was really being honest and authentic about my feelings. If I wasn't being real, I didn't think I'd ever truly feel safe and secure in my life. Learning this got me excited about my limbic system and emotional brain, and the ways that I could align them with my authentic Affective Self to be as constructive as possible and avoid that hectic stress response.

Emotional Brain

The emotional, or paleomammalian, brain stores highly emotional memories and is where we register our emotional attachments. It is responsible for both learning and motivation, which then influence our behavioral flexibility and Self-development. This emotional limbic system controls our primitive reptilian reactions to our experience and is based on the emotions we allow our Self to feel through our perception.

How we perceive things will most certainly influence how we act.

Depending on what I've been attached to, I may have a destructive emotional reaction rather than a constructive emotional response. Hey, it happens, but I learned it's important to understand the difference.

Destructive emotional *reaction* ← vs. →
Constructive emotional *response*

This is the starting point I encourage you to examine as you decipher your experience. Perception will influence your endocrine system and hormone production, either leaving you relaxed in pleasure, or stressed and in pain.

This limbic emotional brain will be our friend, if we befriend it. It allows us to have impulse control, judge situations, and even demonstrate empathy. It plays an interconnected role with sexual arousal or feeling high from recreational drugs. This part of the brain is core to our Affective Self and is conditioned by previous experiences that shape one's current beliefs. If you can master the experiences felt by the Affective Self, you can thereby control and shape your beliefs, and even how you choose to perceive your experiences.

Focus on how you *feel* during your experiences and understand how you process them. Try to name what you are feeling and ask your Self if you are acting out of instinct rather than intention.

While the Affective Self can identify instinctive, unconscious emotion, you can celebrate that you have an intellectual state beyond your primal one. You move from the emotional and survival reptilian brain to the thinking, reasoning brain. The more intentional states of consciousness from this brain apply previously held beliefs to give context to the Affective Self.

Our species is, however, subject to a negativity bias, which means that when situations of equal intensity are encountered, factors of a more negative nature have a greater effect on our psychological state than neutral or positive ones. We notice the bad before we notice the good.

In the moment we experience them, negative emotions are way more destructive than positive ones are constructive. By naming your emotions, you will develop more Self-awareness to monitor your Affective Self and counteract this conditioned negativity bias. This is supported by mindful perception and practicing a constructive emotional response—you can consciously shift perception from negative and destructive to positive and constructive. Don't worry, this is explained in more detail later, but for now, think about it with this example. Have you ever held on to one little comment you felt attacked by, when in the grand scheme of all the things people have said about you, it's actually super tiny in comparison? Yet the comment circulates, syndicates, and creates a spiral of negative association or defensive reactions. The ways we trip our Selves up on the most minuscule happenings of humiliation are attributed to our amplifying the negative and dismissing the greater context.

Remember, perspective is your saving grace. Here and now are what matter. You need to focus on how you keep evolving while leveraging the inevitable negative nature of this life.

So, what is the scale of your negative and positive feelings in your affective state? To look at this, we need to dive deeper into emotions.

Emotions: What Exactly Are They?

I define emotions as the variance of sensations one feels in response to stimuli. Under different sets of circumstances we experience natural instinctive responses that are intuitive. Initially, emotions are not products of our knowledge or reasoning. They are, for the most part, automatic and give us a feeling or inclination to react or respond to our environment in ways that best serve our evolutionary needs.

The Latin derivative *emotere* actually means *energy in motion*, which creates a sensation that is felt. The consciousness of thought applied to the sensation of an emotion to perceive it creates a feeling. I believe emotions come from our subconscious mind as messages to our conscious mind, and the processing of our emotions generates a feeling that is meant to inspire action.

Subconscious mind → Messages sent as emotions →
Conscious mind → Apply thoughts to generate feelings →
Perception → Reaction vs. Response → Experience →
Memory → Beliefs / Expectation

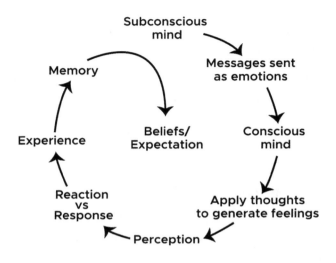

Diagram 2.3

An emotion from a physiological instead of psychological view is just a stimulus looking for a response in an effort to Self-regulate our body. It's the message we receive from our subconscious mind, that sixth sense, our True Self. It creates a sensation that, in turn, motivates us to take action. The more authentic you are about your emotions, the more aligned you will feel with your True Self, and your behavior will reflect that alignment with feelings of happiness, pleasure, and life satisfaction.

Emotions are central to our sensory system and help us stay balanced. They navigate us to the most pleasurable and optimal states.

Remember, the purpose of life is joy, and humans seek to avoid pain and experience pleasure.

I believe we want to do more things to give us that feeling of satisfaction. So, indulge in the mindfulness and presence to stay connected to your emotions and recognize that you can control how you feel about them. Do not demote the priority of understanding the core of what drives your choices; instead, hold space between action and reaction and dominate at behaviors that serve your greatness, as you need to master this part of your Self. Take time to register your emotions and the actions required to address them most constructively. That's what holding space is—it's like hitting the pause button to read the message from your subconscious (i.e., feel your emotion), and then in that space consider what the best response is *before* you act.

Essentially, your emotions aren't all that motivates your actions. They're also driven by your needs, and there is a great overlap here. The emotion of fear, for instance, will lead you to feel you are in danger and your safety needs will become priority, as we saw with Abraham Maslow's pyramid and Theory on Human Motivation (1943). How we satisfy our needs, starting from the base of the pyramid to its peak where Self-actualization takes the pinnacle, is directly related to our emotional state.

Moving up the pyramid demands positive emotional states. The escalation toward Self-actualization relates to a more eudaimonic state of happiness. In this understanding of our psychology, to satisfy our needs and form associated motivations, Maslow claimed that the base of the pyramid would always have its needs met first before progressing toward the needs higher in the hierarchy.

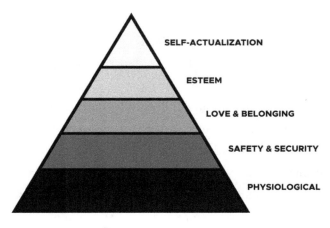

Diagram 2.4

First — Physiological: Air, water, food, sleep, clothing, shelter, sex, homeostasis, excretion

Second — Safety & Security: Personal, financial, health, well-being

Third — Love & Belonging: Friendships, intimacy, family satisfaction

Fourth — Esteem: Achievement, recognition, credibility, respect

Fifth — Self-actualization: Non-judgment, realization of full potential, altruism, morality, unconditional love

If the needs of the first priority are not met, the body will be unable to focus on secondary and tertiary needs. Similarly, if you experience the emotion of fear and feel your safety is in jeopardy, you will not be able to work on your esteem or realizing your potential. I am sure you have experienced this if you have forgotten to eat for an extended period. You reached a point where you couldn't think, communicate, or function until you had something to eat. Or, you had a series of nights with bad sleep, and then you couldn't think about scaling up on more commitments to propel your Self toward success, because you were exhausted. Your basic needs were not being met.

These limitations are created through our emotions and through our perception, as certain emotions are registered as pain by the brain. Subconsciously, we keep our Selves in survival mode simply by leaving emotional pain unaddressed. The resistance or denial of pain is our greatest disservice to metamorphosis.

Where pain is, pleasure cannot be.

They cannot co-exist, and pain will always be prioritized for survival.

This is why, for happiness and life satisfaction, you need to learn how to minimize your pain. The goal is to ensure you control your emotions and perceive them as neutral (or ideally positive and pleasurable) rather than negative and painful. Examine how you use perspective to neutralize destructive emotions. Could things be worse in the grand scheme of things, and are there actually things you can be hopeful about?

I also realized you have to feel you *deserve* happiness. And that starts with Self-esteem.

What Is Self-esteem?

The traditional sense of Self-esteem and its embodiment of Self-worth includes thinking positively about your Self and feeling you deserve respect. Esteem appears in the fourth level of Maslow's Hierarchy of Needs, and this relates to accomplishment, recognition, respect, status, and prestige, which largely rely on external factors. Internally, however, Self-esteem is often defined as what you feel about your Self, your worth, and the way you perceive your own value to the world. It's interesting, because I wouldn't say I was a person with low Self-esteem, but in looking at what Self-esteem is, I actually did have a problem with it. Low Self-esteem has a massive correlation with depression, which we will discuss in the next chapter.

I'm sure you have felt valued in this world at some point, and yet you still feel unworthy.

I've had a successful job and delivered in my roles and responsibilities that contributed to the success of my company. My work satisfied my employer so much, I was named the company Pacesetter in 2016 by American Express Centurion Lifestyle. I was of value and could identify a healthy level of Self-esteem, yet I still struggled to feel like I had a high Self-worth. I would like to explore the worth part further.

I asked myself, *worthy of what?*

Worthiness can relate to love, success, and most of all, happiness. To feel worthy is to feel you deserve happiness. So, a high Self-esteem could indicate a belief that you are worthy of happiness, and that belief can in turn lead to you experiencing happiness because you feel you deserve to be happy. You welcome the perspective of joy.

Several studies show that quality of life and mental well-being are significantly impacted by a person's level of Self-esteem. It's been deemed such a determining factor of well-being and happiness that in the 1980s the California State Legislature wanted to investigate ways to raise Self-esteem among its residents and funded a task force to run this investigation. They believed higher Self-esteem would reduce welfare dependency, unwanted pregnancies, drug addiction, and crime. That's a huge leap, yet, the bill was passed almost without opposition, and the task force ran its operation from 1987 to 1990, with the final report from the operation becoming the highest-selling state document of all time. It sold 60,000 copies.

There were disputes in response to this report, and it's still in question how Self-esteem relates exactly to cultural and socioeconomic factors. But without a doubt, Self-esteem has been found to influence one's individual state of well-being.

When we look at techniques for bridging The Authenticity Gap of Happiness in Chapter 5, we'll discuss how to develop a high Self-esteem. But right now, let's take a look at how your Cognitive "known" Self plays a part in your Self-knowledge and the thoughts and beliefs that influence your Authenticity Gap of Happiness.

THE COGNITIVE "KNOWN" SELF

There are three things extremely hard:
steel, a diamond, and to
know one's self.

—Benjamin Franklin

At the core of your Cognitive Self are your thoughts and beliefs, which shape your Self-knowledge and constitute everything you think you know about your Self. The Cognitive Self is understood through introspection—you have to look inward at your desires and motives for life. Self-perception looks at your behavior and answers the question *what am I like?*

How do you describe your personality and individuality? What are the core beliefs you uphold, and how do you explain your attitude and world perspective?

While Self-esteem looks at the ways you feel about your Self through identifying emotion, Self-knowledge looks at the collection of thoughts and beliefs that create your understanding. Self-knowledge requires Self-awareness to unveil mindset, thinking patterns, belief systems, and reasoning, which make up your Cognitive Self.

Cognition is defined as the act or mental process of awareness, perception, judgment and reasoning, which creates a state of knowing.

The Affective Self is quite primitive compared to the developed consciousness of the Cognitive Self, which can create perspectives from experience. It can analyze the feelings of the Affective Self, create beliefs and values, and develop a sense of morality as it relates to your ability to live a virtuous life. We like the Cognitive Self because it helps us make sense of things, and I believe this dynamic of Self plays a critical role in our ability to connect to more eudaimonic happiness. It helps us think about our purpose and meaning by understanding the core of who we are and what makes us happy in this world. The thought and belief part of Self-alignment and closing the Authenticity Gap of Happiness are largely influenced by your Cognitive Self, and the judgments and perceptions that result from your Self-knowledge.

Thoughts

Thought is the consideration and flow of ideas that comes to mind while the body deliberates between stimuli and a response. They are your non-emotional processes occurring in response to both external, environmental stimuli and internal, emotional stimuli.

Thinking is one of the significant attributes of the Cognitive Self and requires attentiveness. While the Affective Self is instinctive and reactive as per the dominance of the emotional brain and limbic system, the thinking, reasoning, and neocortex part of the brain allows you to perceive, process, problem-solve, decide, and make plans as part of your Cognitive Self. The consciousness of your Cognitive Self is more advanced than the primal, Affective Self, as your thoughts and cognition allow you to learn and acquire new knowledge, develop memory, and use recognition to help you perceive and understand the world. Memory also assists in providing familiarity with experiences and forecasting expectations, and it can even impose a sense of bias to your perception. For example, I know what food poisoning is like, so I have a heightened awareness for expiration dates.

The thing is, when you remember what something was like once, you may expect it to be the same. I've learned that I sometimes need to go into situations with more of an open mind (or so my mom tries to convince me when she offers me expired yogurt).

If you have ever been to a restaurant where the food was bad or the service was terrible, your Cognitive Self determines what you are like in this situation. If you believe everyone deserves a second chance, then you might be open to trying the restaurant again. You might be a bit more optimistic or forgiving, or maybe you just aren't a foodie. If you felt the one experience was enough to turn you off for good, then you will likely also advocate the terrible experience. You swear you will never visit the establishment again, and you demonstrate a more disappointed emotional state. Every experience therefore enhances your Self-knowledge as you discover your preferences, patterns, and processes.

Thoughts lead to cognitive structures, which are relevant because they are the thinking patterns through which you make sense of information. You process information based on your patterns in a way that honors your preferences, and you do this subconsciously.

If you aren't Self-aware of what you're like, can you truly enhance your happiness and pleasure?

It's important to objectively observe your Cognitive Self to ensure you aren't operating from conditioning and close-mindedness. As you seek to evolve your spectrum of life satisfaction, you'll be required to revisit your learned beliefs and cognitive structures. It's never too late to use your perspective to see things from a varying lens of perception.

If you can understand how you think and process your thoughts, you can change your mindset to better shape your expectations and experiences, bridging your Authenticity Gap of Happiness.

Thoughts exist on a surface level as they naturally arise. The fact that we can think about our thoughts is one of the most evolved capabilities of the human brain compared to other species. However, it's also a setback as we can get lost in states of negative thinking, dwelling, procrastination, and resistance.

We need to monitor and organize our flow of ideas and develop positive mechanisms for information processing. Make the choice to perceive with positive emotion, monitor the thoughts that feel good and those that don't, and be willing to explore why. We can filter our thinking so our Self-knowledge and the deep-rooted structure of our Cognitive Self align with positive emotions and pathways to happiness and fulfillment. Again, like with the Affective Self, you can connect to your awareness of a thought, yet detach from giving it meaning if the thought does not serve your joy. If thinking about my Self-worth, doubting my value, and sizing up my life only leaves me feeling despair, I need to find a way to shift my thinking to a more Self-loving space. I need to ask how I can focus on positivity. *What thoughts will benefit me here?*

If you are unaware of negative thinking, this pessimistic mental processing can lead to false assumptions, limiting beliefs, persistent sadness, and despair.

We cannot think bad thoughts and feel good.

Without Self-awareness, we may even end up overlooking the

ways in which we are authentically our Self. Self-knowledge is about figuring out what you're like so you can amplify the good and improve the areas that block your happiness.

People might find you to be defensive, and you may fail to realize you are a person who regularly projects. Projection is a mechanism introduced by Freud in 1895 to explain how we try to avoid being confronted by feelings such as shame. We all inevitably experience emotions such as fear, anger, regret, guilt, and shame, but we must shape our Affective Self to grow in alignment with healthy thinking. This develops a constructive Cognitive Self.

You cannot avoid emotions. You cannot avoid thinking, and you cannot avoid how your emotions and thoughts make you feel. Do not risk developing defense mechanisms, always projecting and blaming others because you never tune into the authenticity of accountability to your Self. I have projected in an attempt to preserve my Self-esteem and to deflect from the destructive emotions that overwhelmed me. It was a way for me to avoid hard truths that were packaged as pain.

Often the emotions and feelings we project indicate how we really feel about our Self. Leaving them unaddressed means they will eventually become a part of our Self-knowledge, identity, and worldview. You have probably seen the parent who never reached their aimed level of success and now reprimands their child with intensity and obsessive attention to performance. This can leave the child discouraged instead of motivated. We have to be aware that projecting cannot right our wrongs. Focusing your energy in this way is not something I recommend.

Projecting will not relieve you of your existing pain.

We should not project our feelings and convince others they will never reach their own goals because we failed to do so. Do not embody low Self-esteem to the point that it becomes your mindset and identity. When I have experienced real lows, I have discouraged my own effort toward great ambition, calling it realism, but that was just the package I put my low Self-esteem in. I was actually projecting my belief in my inability to reach my greatest goals.

Repetition of thought patterns creates a level of association where we automatically group thoughts and experiences together, or behaviors and thoughts together. When we have attention placed where it has always been and that place keeps us out of alignment, then it's time to break the mold. We need to question our default patterns and ask what the similarity and comfort of our life is doing to provide happiness in our day-to-day experiences.

Contiguity is a principle in cognitive psychology. It states that ideas, experiences, and memories become linked the more frequently they are experienced together. These links don't even need to be reinforced; the stimuli and response just need to be frequently experienced together. These links and mental associations then become a part of our Self-knowledge and our Cognitive Self. You think the world is a certain way because of this contiguity. However, if wrong ideas and experiences are merely ingrained through repetition to create your beliefs about the world or your Self, what happens if you link the wrong things?

If we keep having the same negative thoughts about our Self-esteem and keep registering experiences with those thoughts in mind, our memory will create a destructive association. For example, one might think of giving a presentation or doing a performance review, and because their memory of their last review was repeatedly associated with low-esteem thinking, they now fear or even anticipate the next one will be poor also. When trying to fund a feature film, I talked to twenty potential investors with little traction. I could have just written off capital-raising as impossible, because the more I experienced a "not interested," the more likely I was to expect that response. I knew I could not let my Self think about the situation based on what was or had been—instead I had to look at it with the optimism of what could be, and that's how I maintained my excitement. This is what the power of an open mind can do. Being flexible in your thinking doesn't restrict you to limiting patterns; it actually opens you to more opportunities.

If you even say something as simple as *I am so lazy because I always snooze*, then eventually, when you experience pressing the snooze button, you are reinforcing the thought of laziness through action. Then it becomes part of your Self-concept. You feel lazy simply by the continuity of thinking as a lazy person, and it then becomes a part of how you identify your Self. If you condition your Self to associate the sound of the alarm with new thoughts, like *I am disciplined* or even *I am productive early in the morning*, then you will eventually have a cognitive structure that processes your stimuli—the alarm—with a response that best aligns with your thoughts and beliefs. Positive reinforcement in your mindset inclines you to act with discipline. It's actually quite remarkable how powerful positive thinking can be in driving behavior. As a result of the alignment among your thinking, your beliefs, and your behavior, you are left feeling happy.

Beliefs

Beliefs differ from thoughts in that a thought is anything that comes to mind and considered during a flow of ideas. You may not hold every thought to be true, whereas beliefs are thoughts you hold as truth.

Beliefs differ from facts in that you can assume and feel something to be so true, yet it could actually prove itself false.

The perception of certainty is where you believe your thoughts are true, but the actuality of truth may differ. Your beliefs and how you gauge your own truth are completely subjective.

We have all believed things that simply are not true and details that are just not facts. I personally thrive on the truth, but I give equal consideration to the fact that people will have a different opinion of what truth is. I can hold space and agree to disagree. I don't know if it's because we experienced a system that emphasized being right, but people have an attitude of needing to be right in this world. How lovely it is sometimes to just be OK with having different beliefs. Instead of trying to agree with everyone, try to agree with your inner truths and how you shape your Self-concept. If you do not believe in your Self, your worth, your ability, and your value, then I can safely say you will struggle to find happiness, even if you are right most of the time. Start to question your beliefs much like we discussed questioning your thinking patterns. Use the good old *why* analysis: *why do I believe what I believe?*

The repetition of thoughts, as well as experiences in alignment with those patterns of thinking or cognitive structures, create your beliefs, which in turn influence your expectations in the world. It's almost like a Self-fulfilling prophecy, where you expect something to be a certain way, so you think in terms of those expectations and then you evaluate the world to find supporting evidence for your beliefs.

This is known as the confirmation bias, where you not only search for and interpret information in order to confirm your beliefs, but you also recall, sometimes inaccurately, information to support your belief system.

The ways in which your unconscious selection of information pulls on that which reiterates your existing beliefs means you could be overlooking new and valuable information. We evolve our perception by detaching from what we know and expect and instead obtain knowledge from what is actually happening. This is the concept of living in the moment, feeling and observing our Selves in the now.

When you have held a set of beliefs for a long time, it will be a little difficult to change them, so be gentle on your Self. It will require thought alteration and the repetition of those new thought patterns before they become the ingrained set of new beliefs. You will be rewarded when you notice a shift in the Cognitive Self that is more flexible and liberated, releasing attachments that may have held you in suffering or struggle.

Whenever I tried to change and experienced setback after setback, I realized I probably did not find the root of the belief that was driving my mindset and behavior. I could not achieve change without some level of discomfort, but it would have been much more uncomfortable to remain the same and be distressingly out of alignment.

When my thoughts, beliefs, feelings, and actions were at war with each other, I was at war with my Self.

Beliefs create a significant impact on my motivation, and thereby my actions. Even when I developed a positive mindset, attitude, and belief system, I still needed to take action in alignment with those things in order to bridge my Authenticity Gap of Happiness. It was impossible for me to bridge the gap without addressing my beliefs.

Do you believe you deserve wealth? Do you believe you are capable of accumulating prosperity and reaching your financial goals? Do you feel worthy of love? Do you believe you can enjoy a supportive, exhilarating, and balanced relationship with a life partner? Do you believe you can control your health and longevity? The body will listen to what the mind believes, and of this I am completely certain. We will cover this mind, brain, body relationship in Chapter 4.

For now, evaluate what you believe about your Self, your Self-esteem, and your Self-efficacy. These beliefs are important in reprogramming your cognitive structures for a happier, healthier life filled with satisfaction, because they help bridge the gap. New views of your Self will emerge as you start to observe and improve your Self-knowledge.

The Phenomenon of Emergent Self-Knowledge

To understand the existing structure, systems, and security of life as we know it, we make assumptions and uphold certain truths. This is how cultural and societal norms are developed: there is a consensus of beliefs across communities. By foreseeing safety and our survival, we thereby remain sane, knowing our needs will be met.

Beliefs hinge on our ability to predict stability. There is an element of addiction to having our expectations met. We are almost always measuring an experience against what we expect it to be in the moment, or against the result after the fact. Being able to fulfill expectations keeps our minds tame.

Have you ever noticed how uncertainty keeps you on edge? Are you always trying to determine what things will be like ahead of time? By being able to make sense of things, predict, and have certainty in outcomes, we feel a sense of control and safety. We need to realize, however, that we are in a constant state of unforeseen circumstances. Nothing is guaranteed, so the more we treat life as a discovery, balancing intention of outcome with detachment from needing to control it, the more we are in a golden state. This balance allows an element of curiosity to position our Self in a continuum of fascination.

How do you find your own voice? How do you explore your own understanding? How do you give your life meaning from the things you experience?

You just have to be honest, and maybe that feels like you need to have courage.

It takes a lot to think for your Self, to have an opinion, and to articulate your thoughts and worldview. The freedom to think for our Selves is probably one of the best things we will ever have the privilege of doing, so we should enjoy it.

Ariel Phillips, a psychologist and co-founder of the Harvard Success-Failure Project, said something interesting on failure and authenticity when I interviewed her, and I will never forget it.

She said, "To be fully human really depends on who is defining it, but to me, it has to at least include the ways in which we inevitably are in the world. If we accept that we aren't robots or machines, our understanding will be emergent; we will be discovering things as we go along that we couldn't have seen ahead of time."

That statement has since encouraged a motion which I call the phenomenon of emergent Self-knowledge. We are ever-evolving amidst the unpredictability of our circumstances. To be human is to be both a creator and a product of our own transformation, influenced by the universe of volatility that is our world.

I would encourage you to have a mind that is open enough to discover your life, and to consider a different perspective. Are you attached to your beliefs in a way that enforces limits on your life? What about your beliefs around work ethic and the ways in which we enforce an exhaustive focus on meritocracy? I personally decided it's not about competing against one another. Instead, I compete with the previous Gi Gi. I compete against my own potential and capacity for greatness. Self-actualization has nothing to do with you in comparison to others—it is actualizing the potential of your Self.

At some point, we believe that having twelve- to fourteen-hour days means we are hard-working and we are valued. But what if I only work five hours a day, earn more, feel happier with better relationships, and have more freedom and flexibility? This is my schedule because I believed this was the life I could create. My actualization invigorated me into many sixteen-hour days of flow, happily.

You are what you focus on.

If you focus on the belief that a sixty- to eighty-hour work week determines value and worth, then that is what your life will become. You think your circumstances into existence, by focusing on the hours, not on your worth. From this mindset, how long you work becomes the point of attention rather than the value you add, or the qualifications that determine your worth. It's not just you—most of us are constantly trying to maintain the status quo even when it feels like it's driven by obligation instead of inspiration. We really need to know what we value, and we need to align our thoughts, beliefs, and actions with that authentic version of our Self.

Your worth is a matchmaking affair, pairing your internal core values with the external value you contribute to others.

Show Me Your Values, I'll Show You Your Future.

Values are principles that guide our behavior to maintain a standard of character. Attitude is a reflection of our beliefs and values and is portrayed in tone, body language, and expression of Self. It's not just the action we take; we create our attitude with our behavior and the emotions that underlie our actions, which also hinge on our values and beliefs. Below, I will put a statement and you will have an opinion. Do me a favor and ask yourself why you have this opinion and where it came from. This exercise is just to create an awareness of your beliefs, your attitude, and your response to each sentence. It's a discovery technique to uncover some of our values by provoking opinions.

Answer honestly by instinct. Do not overthink these.

- To be a good parent, son, or daughter, I need to spend a certain amount of quality time with my relatives.
- The more friends I have, the more loved I am.
- I need a university degree to be successful.
- Life is significantly easier for people who have good looks.
- Women will become the highest-paid executives in the world in all industries.
- There is no God.
- The average Asian is less educated than the average American.
- All news is controlled by the government and filtered in a way to manipulate and brainwash the audience.
- Orgasms are as good as you make them; your partner has little to do with it. It's all in your head.
- The legal system is fair to everyone and always does the right thing for humanity.
- You can cure disease with a vegan diet, even cancer and diabetes.
- Politicians are the most Selfless humans to exist. They are heroes.
- Interracial couples are trendy.
- People of the same ethnicity will have a better marriage than mixed couples.

- Death by stoning for homosexuality should be allowed in all countries.
- Prison provides lessons in good moral conduct.
- Nonprofit employees should be able to make a good salary.
- Killing dogs for food is the same as killing pigs for pork.
- There is a double standard for the number of sexual partners acceptable for a woman compared to a man.

The point of these statements is not to be right or wrong, but to show how automated our beliefs are. They influence our thinking, judgment, expectations, and most notably, our attitude. There is a social psychology theory called System Justification Theory, and it states that people will satisfy their underlying individual needs by defending or justifying the status quo even when the system may be detrimental to the individual. So, you will hold firm to beliefs that serve your need for stability and inclusion, and be resistant to change if it will contradict the ideologies of the group. You do not want to be cast away from the group, so you protect its beliefs even if deep down you may not be 100 percent aligned with them. Our group, circle, tribe, or squad has an influence on our Cognitive Self, and on what we think, believe, and value.

Show me your friends and I will show you your future.

Make sure your beliefs are not holding you back from outgrowing the average. Make sure you are brave enough to challenge the status quo and to transcend beyond limiting relationships. Greet change not with fear, but with courage. Do not let the fear of being outcast create the discomfort of stagnation as you idle in despair, not reaching your true happiness. I did it, and it isn't all it's cracked up to be. I would rather be authentic and alone than out of alignment and in a group.

A stable status quo with a heartbeat that thrives on our sacrifice to be happy with our Self is not a system worth safeguarding.

If you feel life has become boring and unsatisfying, then the safe path and staying comfortable to avoid pain has maybe reached its expiration. It would be ridiculous to ignore one of our most powerful evolutionary warnings, fear.

Know that you can greet the discomfort of fear and in the face of it, choose courage.

You are where you are now, and you know that you could be happier. To get more out of life requires some type of change. What do you think is keeping you where you are, and how long have you wanted more out of life?

Be observant of your beliefs and ask if you are merely on autopilot, sustaining a system that serves Self-image, group image, and status. Stagnation is easy; change requires chutzpah and a willingness to be uncomfortable. The passive ease around keeping things the way they are will breed regret deep down inside, because you know you could be getting so much more out of life.

Close the gap.

We need to let go of being obsessed with serving our ego and serving the system that keeps the ego intact.

Do not allow it to be your master anymore.

The system reinforces our submissive service through judgment and fear of being unworthy, fear of being unloved, fear of being outcast, and fear of losing what we have, instead of excitement about what we could gain. We believed the jargon and adopted beliefs that diminished our radiant individuality. And then, our jobs became our identities.

Many of us were left dissatisfied and unfulfilled.

Enough is enough.

The purpose of life is joy.

You have a birthright to authentic happiness.

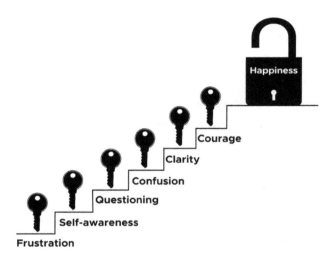

Diagram 2.5

THE EXECUTIVE "ACTIVE" SELF

The Executive "active" Self focuses on the perception of our ability, performance, and at its core, on the behavioral element of Self. When we act in ways that do not uphold our beliefs or how we expect we should act, then we are left out of alignment and experience an Authenticity Gap of Happiness.

The confidence we have in our ability is measured through our Self-efficacy, a term first introduced in 1977 by Albert Bandura, a Canadian-American psychologist. How we choose to act, and how we control those actions and Self-regulate, are decided by the Executive

Self. For instance, if you sacrifice hedonic happiness in the pursuit of eudaimonic happiness by not eating dessert for one month to hit your goal weight and achieve health goals for the purpose of living a longer life, that decision is controlled by your Self-efficacy and Executive sense of Self. The elements that matters most here are the behavior you undertake, the ability to endure short-term pain for long-term gain, and the essential ways in which you can control temptation and delay gratification. These types of executive actions play out in relationships, career, mental and physical health, and are all elements that impact our ability to bridge the gap.

Think about the ways in which Self-efficacy can impact us in times of stress or duress because we have confidence in our ability to control our behavior. If we do not believe in our ability, we might freeze, or we might react aggressively or impulsively rather than developing a healthier active response. Often, high Self-efficacy is linked to resilience, ability to handle adversity, healthy habits, high performance, and achievement. That's a lot of upside.

The Affective Self identifies circumstance and stimulus. In addition, we use our Cognitive Self and reasoning to analyze our Self-knowledge, then use our Executive Self to best decide how to act. Hopefully you are starting to see how Self-esteem, Self-knowledge, and Self-efficacy are interconnected elements of Self. Alignment of these three Selves and your emotions, thoughts, beliefs, and behavior creates the roadmap to close the gap and obtain the happiness you deserve.

If you have a high Self-esteem and for some reason you did not uphold the actions to align with that high Self-efficacy, your Self-knowledge changes. If you continuously act in ways that are out of alignment, you eventually alter your beliefs about your Self. You question if you are who you think you are, worth what you hope you are worth, and capable of the goals you have set for your Self. I've been there.

When I didn't do what I said I would, I ended up in emotional turmoil. I've since learned that keeping my word protects my alignment.

Being out of alignment with the interconnected elements of Self is the easiest path to a destructive Self-concept. Try to avoid threatening mental attitudes, as many of the decisions by our Executive Self are influenced by our Affective and Cognitive Selves.

Do you experience short-fused emotions like anger and blame, or do you project your feelings through defense mechanisms? Your Affective Self drives behavior, so consider what motivates your perception. Are you experiencing spite or jealousy?

There are Self-image implications when we leave low Self-efficacy unaddressed. For instance, if we don't believe we can uphold our health goals, it's more than likely that we will end up bingeing and eating everything that isn't on our list of approved foods. We do this because our low Self-efficacy imprints the beliefs that we are incapable of achievement, so why even keep up the effort. This then reinforces a low sense of Self-worth, impacting esteem and again reinforcing Self-knowledge, because our idea of our Selves has been amplified with actions that affirm that view of Self.

What you believe you are capable of matters.

What you think matters.

What you do matters, even the small stuff.

To have a high Self-efficacy is already a step in the direction of happiness, but that alone is not enough. Prioritize behaviors that reaffirm those beliefs to strengthen your Self-confidence. Much like repetition of thinking leads to cognitive patterns that drive you toward happiness, repetition of aligned actions will do the same. We develop states of happiness through learning and trying new things, and healthy Self-efficacy gives us the confidence to take action outside of our comfort zone.

Remember, the joy is in the journey.

We do not need to have outstanding performance to prove to others we are worthy. That is ego. We should act because it is in alignment with our true desire for experience and because we are confident our experiences will leave us feeling emotionally positive. Otherwise, perhaps you don't take action, return to your Cognitive state, and evaluate which actions bring you joy.

Self-efficacy gets us to take action, and the outcome of that action has implications for the three Selves. While Self-esteem and the views of one's worth seem to be more stable and permanent, a person's Self-efficacy is isolated to the performance at hand. If, for instance, you have high Self-efficacy, you lean into difficulty rather than shy away from it. You are more inclined to greet challenges with optimism. If you underperform, you can use your high Self-esteem to view that performance as an isolated instance of failure. You realize it's not a reflection of your worthiness or value, rather it is learning and progress.

To ensure we are leveraging all elements in the complex feedback loop that is our Self Concept, we should aim to align the three Selves and their respective elements:

- Emotions, the Affective Self and Self-esteem
- Thought and beliefs, the Cognitive Self and Self-knowledge
- Behavior, the Executive Self and Self-efficacy

With emotional illnesses like depression, there is a learned helplessness theory, which can be attributed to the perceived lack of control over one's situation. When looking at the powerful ways we can treat psychological disorders, I believe Self-concept and the three Selves are one of the most essential areas of consideration. Everything about our decision-making and Self-control comes down to your ability to first know your Self.

Treat each with equal importance.

DESPAIR
AND
DEPRESSION

―――

*I first needed you to understand happiness
and your Self in order to understand depression. If you
don't know what either of those things are, depression
can feel too complex and vague. The reality is,
if we don't unpack our baggage, we will eventually break
from carrying it. If we do not understand despair,
we cannot fully treat others with compassion.
For love to thrive in this world and for us to be
happy, we all benefit from understanding
what's behind the hate.*

I HATE IT WHEN THE CURTAINS OPEN, BUT JUST slightly less than I hate leaving the bed. I've lost track of why I should even interact with life. What's the bloody point anyway, right?

I patiently wait to feel any inkling of interest. I am diligent in my slumbersome solitude. It's just an AWOL situation; I am simply absent without leave. The tickle of ambition that used to get me up before sunrise faded so fast without warning.

I am just sleeping my way through this "rough patch." I don't remember how I was the girl I managed to be just days, weeks, and many years before this moment.

I dominated, always.

I set goals, I tried, I failed.

I never hesitated to adjust the sails and keep moving forward. Just fail forward, learn something from it, and it won't have been a waste of my time. The investments that had fallen through, the money that had been stolen from escrow, the husband whose loving hands turned with rage. I laid there, intellectually hardened by life.

I grow accustomed to my tight chest. It might just be dehydration or low blood pressure. Sure, it's that again. I should take it easy, I should rest. I look at messages as if responding to them would be like producing an article for Harvard. It's daunting. The "Hey Gi, how are you?" is now loaded, it's dangerous. It fires at me from a space of cuteness and lands in my cognition as an explosive.

I could write back, "I'm fine," but I've never been one to lie to myself, so I don't write anything at all. Wearing denial like a haute couture ensemble was never my cup of tea.

I am not fine.

Yet still, I will not say I'm depressed.

Daunt Me, but Do It Quietly.

This word *depression* lives a double life between nonchalantly being used, and at other times being dramatized. To say the least, it has dabbled in being taboo and has played as a scapegoat for emotional hardship, laziness, or something so overwhelming in nature that people don't know how to greet the topic. I think it might be helpful to clarify just what depression is, because it is none of the above.

Most people en route to depression will experience despair, which is also debilitating but does not completely hinder your day-to-day capability. I guess I have to ask, would I rather be a functioning person who is terribly unhappy, suffering or struggling, or would I rather be useless in depression? I don't think one is worse than the other because both of them are unhappy, and there is a devastating lack of joy in life, which no one should have to experience. So, from here forward, anything in the painful, life-inhibiting, suffering and struggling capacity that is nonclinical will be labeled as depression, and talking about it matters.

Depression is a mood disorder that is naturally unstable, meaning it can change from time to time and is inconsistent in how and why it prevails. Self-esteem, however, can remain unchanged for an entire lifetime. Low Self-esteem is stable unless given the attention and care to improve it. Depression, being a bit more volatile, can be unpredictable in how it comes and goes.

Why does it matter?

It's the leading cause of disability worldwide, so the relevance of deciphering depression and its significance in understanding your Self and the people in your life can only increase in importance. The economic impact of approximately $210 billion per year is a statistic that stretches beyond the boundary of boardrooms into homes, personal lives, and families. Parents are losing children to suicide, friends are losing their peers, and even children themselves face the unimaginable loss of their heroes.

A business's bottom line is impacted by people coping with depression, but the bottom line is addressing depression is important for our entire world.

Depression is a greatly under-addressed burden, manifesting as problems with education, rising rates of unemployment, and absent people growing physically numb in an overstimulated world. Its daily disguise disables you from the simple life right of feeling happy.

But, what exactly is it?

I guess the most confronting term used for it is "mental illness". You leap with aid and concern for physical illness; if your physical body is in pain, you experience distress and attentively care for it. Perhaps we can attribute the same care to the one driving force of our reality: our mind in all its power.

Without good mental health, we cannot have good reactivity to stimulation. We cannot apply positive thinking, which allows perceptions that drive desired feelings and life experiences. Without good mental health, we cannot master being our Self—we hinder our greatest talents and the potential to Self-actualize.

Without the health of the mind, what type of life are we living?

The mind, after all, is the processing center that dictates the culture of every single thing we experience. The Cognitive Self persuades you into or out of action, making you capable of the impossible through your Executive Self and its beliefs in your capacity to take such action. Your mental health is where it all begins, in the power of your perception and the emotional undertone of your feelings and the Affective Self.

The relevance of this is not restricted to those with depression. It expands to include any individual who struggles with simple joy, sustaining motivation, finding inspiration, and having their life expectations and life experiences align in synchronicity. This applies to anyone who is trying to understand and close their Authenticity Gap of Happiness.

Where does depression start?

If you are feeling an air of unattributed sadness that consistently lingers or won't budge, and you cannot quite put your finger on the why, then this could be an indicator of a depressed emotional state. Sometimes we blame the moon cycle, Mercury retrograde, tiredness, hormones, or just about anything that allows us to stay comfortable in an unexplainable down mood, but depression doesn't always come as a result of a trigger.

Pay attention to your mood. If you are simply uninterested and stimuli, despite their greatest attempts, lack an ability to motivate or excite you, then beware. If you become nonresponsive and your care to perceive life diminishes, then proceed with caution.

I thought there was a whole marathon of down moods to be lived before I reached depression. I thought there would be a climb up an emotional Mount Everest and a trek through the Sahara Desert of negativity.

I completely underestimated how much it can just ambush you.

Feel it, own it, tell your Self the truth.

If you are a far cry away from anything that resembles happiness and life satisfaction, be wary of your vicinity to depression. If you are lucky, you simply get out of this disinterest with ease, but if you are anything like me, the nature by which depression escalates embodies a questioning of one's own worth and life. The really heavy thinking happens when you start to wonder if life itself is worth it.

Don't lift those heavy thoughts as if they are feathers. Don't carry on until they break you.

If we aren't careful, everything can become a mirror of the disgusting inadequacy that is a conditioned life view. Our Self-esteem lowers, our Self-efficacy is jaded, and we simply fail to recognize who we are, what we desire, and even what happiness is. Feeling like a failure, ashamed and never good enough, unworthy of love, and incapable of feeling life's hedonic happy pleasures becomes the new normal. Then you begin *hating yourself for hating yourself*, and you'll use your extraordinary conscious evolution and intellectual capacity to think about this thought.

The vicious cycle continues of decaying in depression, unless we can recognize it in our Self and in our loved ones:

- Weight fluctuations
- Low energy
- Problems concentrating and lack of focus
- Anxiety
- Loss of interest, hope, enthusiasm
- Constantly living in a past already lived that cannot be changed
- Anger issues, easily irritated
- Feeling slow, restlessness
- Sleep disturbance, sometimes excessive sleep that still feels insufficient
- Exhaustion
- Feeling worthless

- Guilt around your choices, difficulty in making decisions
- Suicidal thoughts
- A desire to die

Depression appears in many mutations, with some short-lived and others situational. Sometimes it galivants on its way, never looking back at the debris it leaves. Circumstances change, and the darkness lifts. We recover instantaneously until it pops by the next time. Unmanaged, it can last long after the situation has reached its end.

Remember my best friend Rose from Chapter 1? Well, her husband was diagnosed with stage three bowel cancer, and it threw us into a spin. I learned a lot from Rose about how depression can vary based on the Self and circumstances. She said:

I really hit rock bottom and had to find my way back to myself. I have always been an incredibly happy, positive, and fun person until my now-husband got diagnosed with cancer. I spent nine months helping him get through chemo. Back then, we were not married yet and had only been dating for a few months when he was diagnosed. I love him more than he knows, and my focus was to get him through chemo and get him healthy. In the process of doing this, I forgot to look after myself. I stopped working out, my job suffered, I forgot what I loved to do. I became very insular and didn't have a lot of energy to deal with external things. I lost myself. My husband's cancer stole my life, and I was no longer happy or positive. I became someone I didn't recognize in the mirror, and that was hard.

I stopped finding the joy in life which, if you knew me you would know I can pretty much find the joy in everything. Cancer sucked. It wasn't happening to me, but I let it destroy me. I had no problem sleeping and would definitely oversleep. I found it difficult to get out of bed. Anxiety was the hardest mountain to climb; I couldn't cope. Every day, I was in pain. It became so intense that I would just cry from being completely overwhelmed. And this all happened after Rich got better—he got better, and I got mentally sick. He went back to his life, and I fell apart. I had nothing to obsess with anymore, so then I started believing everything was wrong with me. Was it cancer, was I sick? I lived in constant fear. There was a point where I didn't know if I would ever get better.

After a while, it became clear to me that I wasn't just stressed out. I was having daily crying sessions, panic attacks, and anxiety episodes. To this day, my psychoanalyst maintains I was not depressed. I was suffering from an overwhelming anxious episode that affected my daily life. However, I maintain that I was dancing with depression and didn't fully know how to pull myself out of this rut. Every time I tried to leave the house, I'd have an anxiety attack, or my heart would start racing. Then I would feel incredibly overwhelmed, which would make me cry.

Instead of going out, I'd stay in and watch a movie. Or if I took my dog Winston to the park for a run, I'd have a palaver of emotions, mostly negative. I forced myself to go because I loved Winston so much and I wanted him to enjoy his day. Every time I went to the office, I'd have a panic attack. I hated crowds. The anxiety grew and grew, and eventually I stopped wanting to participate in daily activities. I wasn't aware of it until I completely broke down.

Your body has an amazing ability to pool all of its resources and fight, but at some point, even your body can't give anymore, and that's when it all falls apart. Everything broke down, and that's when I knew I was in trouble. I couldn't lie to myself anymore. Rich got me help and slowly, very slowly, I found my way back.

I wouldn't even call it a mental breakdown. I would call it a Self breakdown.

I lost my way, I was unhappy, and I was feeling guilty for being unhappy. I didn't know how to love myself anymore, so how could I love anyone else? I had to rebuild myself from the ground up. It was a daily journey, but I am so happy I put in the work, because after some hard work I started to slowly feel like me again.

My decision to start seeing a therapist and practice daily meditation was the turning point. Slowly but surely, I returned to the things I loved—working out, meeting up with friends—and my passion slowly came back to me. I had to put in a lot of work mentally and physically. My awareness tripled, my ability to empathize increased, and every day became a little bit easier.

No one ever said life was easy, but they did say it was worth it, and I choose to have a life worth living.

The details of Rose's story are similar to my story, and to you and your story. It is the story of pain left to its own devices, and how the Self gets destroyed.

DEPRESSION AND THE SELF

As with Rose and many other people who find themselves in the mix of despair, anxiety and/or depression, there are a few prominent areas to understand. The tripod of depression I wish to focus on includes:

- **Unresolved emotional trauma** and the Affective Self look at what depression *feels* like to you, what painful attachments you have yet to resolve, and what *emotions* your suffering manifests as most.
- **Self-defeating mental habits** and the Cognitive Self address what depressive *thoughts* you are having, what *beliefs* your pain

is rooted in, and the damaging conditioned Self-knowledge that leaves you disliking your Self.

- **Lack of life vision** and the Executive Self, highlighting how you *act* when you are depressed, what unhealthy *behavior* is adopted, the destructive choices you are making, and fixing the ways in which your loss of interest and motivation is destroying your life.

Unresolved Emotional Trauma

Unresolved emotional trauma looks behind the curtain. It opens the closet to check out the skeletons. It's our baggage. This is the trauma that can make us reactive, unrealistic in judgment, impulsive, and feel we are in turmoil. It will get us to do anything to numb the pain.

How heavy is your baggage?

If we did a bit of emotional Magic 8-Ball, it would go something like this. Take a walk down memory lane. For a moment, close your eyes and take a few deep breaths (actually do it) and visualize your life. Start with what you discuss in confidence with your closest friends. Are there things you continuously revisit, but nothing has changed? Do you keep re-assessing something already done and dusted? You actually know you should be moving on from it, but somehow your headspace can't seem to get the distance it needs. Even when you finally move on, are there painful memories you always seem to face, or that you get triggered to remember? And when the memories surface, you feel like it's happening all over again?

Are you still angry about unresolved issues in a relationship? Do you have guilt for something you did, or regret for things you didn't? Do you still feel cheated or mistreated by friends, colleagues, or loved ones? What's happening in your work life that's pissing you right off?

What's happening with your ex, and why can't you stop stalking their social profiles or replaying what went wrong? Do you have money problems, counting down the days until payday or avoiding the credit card bill? Are you lonely? Or perhaps you're a heavyweight champion of mentally beating yourself up with harsh Self-judgment and a negative Self-image, constantly wishing you looked different?

Don't worry about the fact you are struggling with things that you think others will find insignificant. Trust me when I say this: we have all been there, and it's time we own it.

Give yourself permission to acknowledge your pain.

Acknowledge the load you have been carrying. Let it all surface. This is a safe space, and doing this exercise seems confronting, but it is powerful.

Discovering Your demons:
Come Out, Come Out, Wherever You Are!

From our little visualization and emotional eight ball, we now have a range of things racing in our minds. Write them down. Write down each and every pain point and struggle. Don't overthink, and don't be shy. This is not a time to hold back on your list of pain and struggle.

It doesn't make you a victim or weak. It makes you brave and honest.

When you see this list, it's going suck because you will see, right there in front of you, a reflection of how much you have been harboring. More than that, some of it is going to seem batshit irrational, and that's actually a good thing.

Like food that's poisoning your system, better out than in.

Think about how you reacted the last time things went wrong. Think about the last time you were hurt or disappointed by someone or lied to. Think about what makes you angry at yourself—the feelings you just can't seem to budge. Evaluate your behavior and how you hate on yourself for the vices you cannot overcome.

Listen, we can't solve a problem if we don't acknowledge its existence.

It's time to fess up or stay fucked. We did not come this far to only come this far. I'm here with you and can tell you the more honest you are, here and now, the more happiness, pleasure, life satisfaction, and success you will achieve after this process.

Now that you have your list, imagine taking out some suitcases. Lay them down and open them so you have them empty and ready to pack. You then receive a delivery of about 100 black eight-balls for a game of pool. For every single thing on your list, pack an eight-ball. Anything that doesn't make you feel good and is making you feel bad, for every destructive emotion in each memory, pack an eight-ball. If you think one ball isn't enough because the trauma is so severe, pack two eight-balls.

All packed. Great. Take a deep breath!

If you actually did write out this list and you envisioned how many suitcases and balls you would pack, then you feel like you might have a lot of unresolved emotions and you don't know where to start.

If you zipped those bags up and tried to carry them around for an entire day, it would be debilitating. Imagine you take these suitcases *everywhere*; the bathroom, shower, bed, shopping, the office, wild night out, the gym, playtime with the kids, a nice weekend getaway, and for some sexy time under the sheets. This wouldn't be the baggage you want to be carrying around, would it? It would literally be back-breaking.

Yet somehow we do this to our Self, ignorantly carrying emotional baggage that unconsciously weighs heavily on our ability to obtain the life we deserve.

Over time it will chip away at us, showing up as stress, restlessness, short fuses, and snappy attitudes.

Eventually that emotionally blocked pain and unresolved trauma manifests itself in physical ways. We get tension knots, experience anxiety, suffer sleep disorders, and eventually our mental health will turn into more serious physical and sometimes life-threatening illnesses. Destructive emotions that have not been balanced leave the body in such a toxic state of stress they become malignant. You are no stranger to your demons' best friend: stress, the silent killer.

I care for you too much to let you wither away in illness, mental or physical. Knowing how you can identify your emotions, name them, embrace them, and constructively shift them will be a huge part of bridging the gap, and that exciting stuff is covered in Chapter 5.

The time of showing you just what happiness is, why you deserve it, and how you can get it is here.

Depression has taken too much from my life, and suicide has taken a handful too many of those I've had to grieve. It's crippling, and often you never realized that you were just on the line between doing OK and losing your Self. The difference is being Self-aware enough to do what you just did—look deep within and face your pain.

This is why authenticity is the value that ignites Self-discovery. It is the flame of vulnerability that lights our path.

If we are unwilling to first admit what we are truly feeling, how the Affective Self is coping, and where our Self-esteem is at, then we can never improve and strive for true euphoric happiness.

Be vulnerable enough to be authentic, because without truth, there is no life satisfaction. If we are not actively addressing happiness, we are risking the path toward despair.

Emotional Equilibrium

As you have learned previously with happiness, there is a hedonic adaptation and, much like positive states return to neutral, we can be thankful that negative states and traumatic emotions will also neutralize as we naturally seek emotional equilibrium. The excruciating pain of an experience should in fact lessen as we adapt to it. However, if the set point is actually despair because we are leaving our emotions unresolved, then we will return to a destructive state as our set point.

The only way we can positively transcend our Affective Self is to be Self-aware. Identify your set point of emotional equilibrium and improve it to heighten satisfaction. You do this by analyzing the consistency of your emotions, your default mood, and the ways you are consistently expressing your attitude.

A proactive approach to feelings of anxiousness requires inner dialogue, asking questions, and Self-reflecting. To truly uncover the root of our emotions, we can apply some positive psychology and reinforce optimistic thinking to change emotion. When we assume bad outcomes, we can instead think about if things did work out in our favor and leverage the power of perspective. Instead of focusing on what could go wrong, we could focus on what could go right.

Another thing I have found helpful to identify pain is to name my emotions. I also use perspective to lessen the magnitude of the pain and affirm to myself the good that can be attributed to it. For instance, I try to find a lesson, a helpful takeaway, or just hold space from a relationship that was actually harmful. It's OK to take a break. If you can be courageous, then change your circumstances; move on to a better career if that's what you know deep down you want. Love each day a little more after you grieve a loss, because it puts life in perspective. Think about the gratitude you have for health on the other side of illness.

What we choose to think about and how we create the perception of our emotions and trauma will inevitably influence the state that we continue to default to. This is why our mindset and Self-knowledge are key to ending despair and preventing depression.

Self-Defeating Mental Habits

Mental habits are the ways in which we have conditioned our information processing and reasoning of thought to perceive and understand our life. Whether we place our attention and focus on positive or negative determines if our mental habits are optimistic or pessimistic. What we observe and how we choose to create context determines whether we are constructive or destructive. We can also be comparative in ways that empower us or defeat us. It was easy when I had low Self-esteem to perceive life inaccurately as I filtered my thinking and beliefs through that lens. I sold my Self a story that I was so much worse off than others.

The confirmation bias is our natural tendency to perceive and favor information in ways that confirm and support our existing beliefs and values. This bias is largely unconscious to the unaware Self. It will cause us to even ignore information that conflicts with our beliefs. Imagine how many things we are ingraining and reinforcing in our mind through the confirmation bias. If we believe we are unworthy of love, we search for evidence to confirm that. If we are lacking Self-confidence, we recall information to support or even defend our shyness. This spans the breadth of all three Selves as we sometimes unknowingly are engaged in Self-defeating mental habits about our Affect, Cognition, and Execution.

We begin to concentrate on all the wrong things. Even as we reflect, the ways in which we understand our Self are irrational and distorted, which leaves us feeling anything but happy. Our confirmation bias and the need to find supporting evidence of our unworthiness, lack of confidence and Self-worth, and expectation of rejection or failure, will eventually lead to a shift in our Self-knowledge. We will falsely filter "evidence" to support inaccurate beliefs. We beat our Self down until we become those new beliefs and truly do have evidence of them.

When we lose our Self-awareness, we lose the ability to monitor and enhance our sense of Self. It happens more easily than you think.

Negativity Bias

If you think the confirmation bias is bad, let's dig deeper into its twisted sibling—the negativity bias. It's another instinctive and evolutionary mechanism that leads us to focus on the negative rather than the positive. I believe it's the catalyst for Self-defeating mental habits. The reality is that when we are exposed to things of equal nature, we will be consumed more by the negative. We notice the negative even when there is something equally positive happening.

Leaving our Self to its default demise would essentially have a result of being over-stimulated by the negative, even in the presence of positive experiences.

Since we cannot stop bad things from ever happening again, we have to disarm this bias.

This is why attention, objectivity, and perspective are so essential to creating a positive state of Self-knowledge. Make an effort to create a perception of life that is geared toward positivity and joy, and you will overcome the cognitive predisposition toward this bias.

Awareness will assist you in being mindful as you perceive situations. When something negative happens, put it in context. Ask why it isn't actually so bad. Ask if there is anything you can actually appreciate about the experience, or if you expanded your knowledge because you learned something new. Is there something positive as a contrast where you are better off focusing your attention?

The Pessimism Bias

While the negativity bias is the Affective Self being amplified by negative rather than positive emotions and is a favorability toward destructive emotions, I believe the pessimism bias impacts our Cognitive Self and expectations in life. Pessimism exists through the belief in bad things happening. There is an expectancy of bad outcomes, and this eventually leads to hopelessness and a sense of frustration. People who are unaware of their pessimistic nature will often give up because they anticipate the worst. They are more prone to depression, and they are less likely to close their Authenticity Gap of Happiness because they simply have a flawed capacity for reasoning.

When our cognitive structures are rooted in pessimism, it becomes difficult to shift our beliefs. We have false beliefs about our Self-esteem, we think we are disliked, and we exaggerate our diminished Self-worth. We project an expectation of failure that gives us low Self-efficacy. We rarely try because of this, and that lack of effort fuels the Cognitive Self into this destructive mindset.

We can easily fall into a discouraged default state, and eventually we will disengage from more parts of our life as we believe the worst outcomes in our career, relationships, and health. We essentially start proving those beliefs in an effort to justify the ongoing pessimism. Like with the negativity bias, we need to break the cycle and take more control of our ability to improve our state of mind. We can put our emotional experiences into perspective by choosing to see opportunity and solutions. We can develop rational and optimistic thinking patterns that will support beliefs that lead to happiness and life satisfaction.

Locus of Control

If we believe that external factors always control our life, then our opportunities and our ability to be happy are in the hands of the external forces that be.

An external locus of control, which goes hand in hand with pessimism and negativity, is when we think everything is happening *to* us, not *because of* us. The Locus of Control was a concept developed by Julian B. Rotter in 1954 and has become an integral part of understanding the psychology of personality and the Self-concept.

Our Self-knowledge needs to be nurtured so that regardless of circumstances, we have control over our perception, response, and ability to find happiness. Central to the internal locus of control is where we attribute our life satisfaction, fulfillment, and our success, as well as our failures and misfortunes. Are you accountable? Do you take that control upon your Self? If you don't, then the time has come to update the way you have been doing things.

Repeat out loud, "I am in control."

Say it a few times.

"I am in control of my life."

Without this control, it is easy to develop anxiety, not feeling safe or stable and not knowing what to expect. Remember our species thrives on comfort zones, stability, and security. Feeling in control helps us feel happiness. Surrender is when we let go of control and make peace that things are out of our control, but it is different than thinking you have no control. When we focus on our internal locus of control, we can take initiative to adjust expectations, pair the right optimistic thoughts and beliefs with our experiences, and bridge the gap.

We might experience pessimism in the sense that we foresee difficulties and distress, but positive pessimism allows us to keep perspective and embrace those hardships with high Self-esteem, knowledge, and efficacy. This happens when we believe we will make it through anything.

I invite you to strive for confidence in your ability to demonstrate emotional maturity, to continue to show up and be active in the ways that will be best for you, even in the face of difficulties. This is done by training your Self to believe that you are capable of dealing with anything that life throws at you, because you are. Affirmations can help with that. I'll discuss those in Chapter 5, but for now, you can prepare for hardship by being open to your own accountability.

Listen to the defeat and say, "No more. No more Self-defeating thoughts." Mindfulness will aid you in being aware if you have any negative and pessimistic traits, and through this perspective, you can shape your perception. Improvements are on the horizon.

Especially when things were hard and I was in a state of struggle or suffering, I found myself looking with resentment at those who were thriving. I convinced my Self they had it so much better and so much easier. The Self-defeating mental habit of social comparison can lead to despair.

Social Comparison

To develop our Self-knowledge, we observe the world. While doing that we likely compare our Self to others, our life, status, ideologies, and values. These are all summed up in comparison to how our peers, colleagues, and partners experience life. We compare our Self to the image of a life they let us perceive. The notion that one learns about themself by gaining insight from comparison to their social world is called Social Comparison Theory, a concept introduced by Leon Festinger in 1954. From his work, I think it's not unlikely that we landscape our beliefs, confidence, and ability in comparison to the accomplishments of others.

Hear this: every single human you compare your Self to was once a person with zero experience.

No one in history ran a mile in four minutes until it was done.

If Roger Bannister looked to the existing knowledge and the facts and records of what was possible, he may have actually been discouraged when he set the record in 1954. Through social comparison, others now have seen what is possible, and the four-minute mile has been run by more than 1,400 male athletes.

This element of Self-judgment can serve to discourage you if you make negative comparisons, or inspire you if you are driven to improve. You might relate yourself to someone accomplished, and that provides Self-enhancement and becomes a positive empowering comparison as you idolize and reinforce the success that has been achieved and proven possible. Compare, but use this as a tool and look at the world as a means to inspire, reassure, and drive your Self-knowledge optimistically.

The more you believe in possibility, the more you can leverage your Executive Self and its Self-efficacy to create a thriving life of happiness. To do that, however, you need to have a vision of what you want for your Self, and you have to define your version of happiness.

Life Vision

Vision without action is merely a dream. Action without vision just passes the time. Vision with action can change the world.

—Joel A. Barker

When motivation is lost, efforts diminish and failure ensues.

We can find our Selves in a state of despair, and if we lose hope in life itself, then we've arrived at depression. A major contributor to nonclinical depression is a lack of life vision. Humans are Self-actualizing species, and a part of our evolutionary imprint hinges on wanting to become the best we can be.

On a spiritual level, when we lack life purpose, we lack vision. We have a soul mission and natural talents that create a belief we can do more, have more, and accomplish more. When that potential is left unrealized, we experience distress.

When we do not know what our vision is to start with, we can feel very confused about our life. Inspiration comes and goes, we lack focus, and the grit to persevere is unreliable. We believe we can do more, but we are not taking action. That Authenticity Gap of Happiness burdens us, and if it doesn't, it should.

For me, it's the most unsettling thing to be out of alignment. It's most rewarding when I'm in alignment, because it's where ease, flow, and progress happen.

The importance of who we are and what we can do in this world can easily feel like it's up for question when we don't know what impact we are making, why we matter, and where we fit into the world in a meaningful way. Our purpose or vision and the way we take action in alignment matters if we want to reach the epitome of well-being.

Lack of motivation is one of the leading symptoms of depression. To address depression, we must understand what gets us—and more importantly, keeps us—motivated.

Motivation

Motivation is the drive to take action in an attempt to have a desire fulfilled and pleasure experienced. Short-term motivation aligns with our hedonic happiness. Long-term motivation aims at acquiring eudaimonic happiness and life satisfaction. Our desire to please our Self and internal desires forms our intrinsic motivation.

If we are chronically unmotivated, it could be attributed to a lack of vision and feeling unclear about where to make an effort. If our vision is not truly authentic to our joy, we will stay unmotivated, because the accomplishment of that vision does not align with our authentic emotions and satisfaction. We won't be driven to act if what the action itself accomplishes leaves us with little pleasure.

Sometimes we do things because we feel that we need to.

Sometimes that feels joyful, sometimes it feels sickening.

It's a battle between obligation and passion.

It's the pressure to perform while questioning the purpose.

Breathe.

You need to be sure that you understand what is motivating you and how that aligns with who you are. If you do not know who you are, nothing can really make you truly happy. The goal is to stay rooted in positive motivation rather than pressure to take action. Any motivation is good for people who lack motivation, but there is a right way to motivate yourself. Emotionally, you want to act from a constructive and sustainable state, which allows you to be more inclined to obtain both hedonic and eudaimonic happiness.

The negativity and pessimism biases are certain to keep us from taking action. They squander motivation, because through those lenses of perception, any action we take will lead to a bad outcome. When we have a negative mindset and Self-defeating mental habits, it is hard to believe in our life vision. We need to ensure that we are in a positive state of mind, otherwise finding motivation will be difficult.

If you make assumptions that you will fail or will not experience a good outcome as a result of your action, then you simply will not make an attempt, at least not one worth acknowledging. Don't defeat your Self before you even try. Don't stop your Self from making an effort because you have made an assumption about the outcome. Please do not engage in low Self-esteem, or question your worthiness. Do not be afraid of a bad performance. Also, the sheer size of the vision can deter us from taking the first step. We need to be sure our goals are realistic and achievable in their small steps forward, otherwise our motivation is likely to deteriorate.

Identify, crave, and seek the reward.

Fight for the pleasure that can be found in making an effort. It feels invigorating to win at your goals, to live up to your potential, to chase and catch your dreams.

What you do not find within your Self initially can be ignited externally.

Extrinsic motivation serves to please external forces, such as expectations of others, always wondering how you will be judged, and if you will measure up. This motivates some; it frightens others. We can leverage our social comparison complex, but we should not rely on it, for it is rooted in ego, and where ego is, happiness will flee.

When we only feel good about our Self if we are as good or better than those around us, then we might not be rooted in authentic motives. We are constantly chasing a pleasure that does not deliver fulfillment.

Our state of life satisfaction is rooted in the authenticity of our vision.

Root your Self in purpose.

Do things on purpose.

Prioritize purpose.

If you are achieving, slaying, and continuously chasing, then what you get will be mistaken for happiness when really it is just people showering you with validation. That comes with an expiration date, and you are only left with your Self when the raining praises enter drought.

The Achievement Drive

Some of us feel that we have this obsessive drive to achieve goals. If this pursues in everything we approach, then we ought to check our Self. If we always want to demonstrate the best of our abilities to find acknowledgment and approval, we might be experiencing an unhealthy achievement drive. While constantly dominating our potential is positive, if we are doing it as a means of validation, then we are rooting our motivation in ego.

The last thing that you should want to feel consistently worthy and validated by is ego.

Love me, love me, say that you love me.

For a long time, I felt that I had to achieve great success to be worthy of love. I had to be in the spotlight, in the winner's circle, in the top percentile, otherwise I was unworthy, otherwise I was unlovable.

Some of you may also believe that you have to achieve greatness to feel worthy of love. You might feel so worthy of that greatness that you think your achievement needs to reflect that, but overcompensating with work and obsessing over goals as a means of pleasure or Self-esteem can compromise the balance among your authentic needs.

You need balance.

Your relationships deserve you, not just your work.

Your discipline deserves you, not just your social life.

Your health deserves you, not just your obligations.

You deserve you, full stop.

Becoming obsessed with performance can compromise our psychological and physiological needs if we are not getting enough rest or we start making unhealthy choices because we feel strung out, burnt out, and have little energy to keep up with our basic needs. So many of us run our Selves into the ground, and why?

There is a fear-of-failure epidemic that either leaves us in stagnation or destroys us with overcompensation.

As Ariel Phillips from Harvard also advised me:

> In this population of primarily Harvard students, the Success-Failure Project aims to address concerns on students' own terms, terms that make sense to students. Some students have defined success in such a way that it includes virtually no failures, so their concern might be, "How do I avoid failure altogether?"

This is so common in many of the top schools now as suicide rates rise to match the pressure to achieve.

Be wary and tread mindfully. Ask yourself what you are driven by. It's important. It is not always a lack of life vision that may serve to depress you. Rather, it's the pressure to meet unrealistic standards of perfectionism.

Phillips continues, "Failures and mistakes can impact a sense of Self. I think that's true for a lot of students and also faculty members. As if they are someone who doesn't fail. The problem is that being too afraid of failure inhibits learning, inhibits openness to healthy risks and true discoveries. Students often say, 'I don't want to ruin my perfect record.'"

Sometimes new action needs to precede motivation to break the cycle, to counteract distorted Self drivers, or even hopelessness, and to remind us of our own capability to change. We are what we do repeatedly. Our repeated actions become our habits.

Our brain's neurons wire together, those which more frequently fire together. Every time we take an action, a specific set of neurons related to that action "fires," and the more they fire together, the more they "wire" together. This is when things become easier because the action itself is efficiently and effectively supported by the brain, and it therefore becomes familiar. When we repeat behaviors, we create that path of least resistance and things feel more pleasurable as we generate strong neural pathways through repetition.

Changing habits is difficult not because the new is hard, but because the old wiring is strong.

Our outdated habits across the three Selves need to change in ways that create new neural pathways that serve our vision of happiness. We can create a solid foundation of beliefs that empower our capability to succeed at our vision. Analyze what gets you motivated, but know that you won't always be able to rely on the external, nor should you. The pressure to deliver for others may very well kill you. Instead, you need deep-rooted intrinsic motivation that excites you.

Show up, do the work.

The difference between ordinary and extraordinary is that extra action. Start with your Self-efficacy, and believe that your efforts are going to make a difference. Take action.

Focus on the next step ahead of you. Reaffirm that effort. Stay positive by practicing Self-enhancing thoughts, gear your Self toward high Self-esteem emotions, and develop an approach to learning that is rooted in the optimism of your vision.

You learn by doing. You grow by perceiving.

Do the work.

Sometimes you only learn what you want by experiencing that which you do not want.

Be aware enough to Self-reflect.

Life is trial and error, and there are many things that we try, and then realize they are not a good fit. Sometimes we try and fail at first. We even fail for a second, third, and fourth time.

I've learned to develop grit, and it's helped immensely, especially when supported by a heart of passion and an attitude of perseverance.

If we do not have a life vision that is compelling, inspiring, and rooted in purpose, we can easily slip out of motivation. As you experience hedonic adaptation, remember that initial excitement returns to emotional equilibrium. Motivation that felt like lightning bolts in your body will disappear in a flash.

Where inspiration and motivation might fade, purpose and vision will prevail.

Keep taking action. It feels good when you are growing; the brain thrives and the body enjoys it. Use the brain's motivation-reward mechanism to your advantage by focusing on what you will get when you complete the action. Focus on the impact, the rewards, the joy waiting for you once you get to work and slay. Things will take time. Develop patience and, more importantly, develop a trait that gets you through the downs—Self-compassion.

Self-Compassion

Starting with Self-compassion is important, because there is not a human on earth who will escape mistakes, downfalls, underperformance, failure, setback, grief, or anything that genuinely makes you feel like you could have been better, done better, or deserved better.

The world doesn't set out to destroy you, but it will.

It will, if you let it.

Just eliminating destructive criticism brought me so much relief. It made me feel bad about myself, so I developed an acceptance for who I was in that moment and who I was becoming. I even learned to love the gap that existed as I transcended toward the latter. Allowing myself to simply be my Self was glorious. I did not apologize for not knowing any better, because I knew I was learning and growing.

The other thing I did was treat everyone else with the same compassion. Everyone is on their own journey.

Root your Self in virtuous character—lead.

Lead your life.

Think about your legacy and be brave enough to be remembered for something.

Constructive criticism and Self-compassion means not victimizing your Self in light of circumstances where you have fallen short. On the contrary, it means having a positive regard for your three Selves as you experience your life. To be growing and learning is to be human. You must develop skills. You must learn. Every master was a beginner. You are not born an expert.

Perfection is perception.

Like happiness, perfect is a choice.

There is room for mistakes, error, failure, and if you don't think so, make room. Reflect and fail forward by learning as you grow.

It is your ability to use these experiences to shape your expansion that makes you more powerful. Broaden your Self-knowledge, improve your Self-esteem, and go for it. By keeping your Self rooted in compassion, perspective, and context, you are already at an advantage because you prevail. If you can move past dwelling, then you are already winning. You will maintain momentum and move on to the next things stronger and wiser.

If you are doing it right, there will never be a time when you are not a work in progress, and accepting that will be liberating. You will always and forevermore be evolving your Self; you will always be emerging. That is the joy of life. The privilege to escape boredom is to align with the acceptance that you are here to keep learning.

Where Self-esteem will make you feel worthy, Self-compassion will allow you to deal with suffering in ways that move you into struggling and then thriving. Your Self-talk needs to be rooted in unconditional love as you tune in with gentle nurture to that with which you struggle the most. Self-compassion is believing in your ability to make it through hardship. It is allowing your Self to be less than you had hoped and not hating yourself for it. It is accepting your journey as a constant state of becoming.

Any man or woman who stands in the position you wish to hold was once standing in the position you are in right now. You are evolving, you are reading this, you are showing up, and that's where change begins. This is where you build your bridge.

Some people have done more work to date than you have, some are at the finish line of one transformation, while others are at the beginning, but each and every one of us has to start somewhere.

Grow with grace, be kind to yourself, have empathy for others, but grow.

THE
NEUROPSYCHOLOGY
OF HAPPINESS

*I believe that if the connection
of mind, brain, and body are not understood,
the magic of alignment cannot unlock your
ultimate happiness and potential.
They all must be considered—the psychology,
the neurology, and the physiology.
And what I believe even more is that it isn't
simple, but we can make it so.*

I
NACTION.

Procrastination.

Isolation.

Those are a deadly combination. At a time when it is the world's standard to experience them, those things unify, and they cut me deep. It is not only me; the whole world is on a chopping board.

I stop.

I stop being me, I stop doing the work.

I fade into amnesia.

I don't remember progress.

The only things that hold me are anxiety, debilitating fear, and spinning walls. Unintentionally ignored, I am withering into the realization that I am irrelevant, no one cares, and I do not matter.

I disengage.

I let go from the world, from my vision, from my Self.

During the 2020 lockdowns but before Self-isolation was deadly, the time to "stay home and stay safe" was actually amazing, for me at least.

I had time to myself to get my Self ahead of the game, and I didn't really miss needing to be social. I just finally had some much-needed me time. I went inward, asked deep questions, prioritized health and Self-development, and got clear about how to adapt in a world I was failing to recognize.

I developed a new business plan for an intelligence company and was overly excited about the adventure ahead of me. It almost felt Selfish when everyone was just talking about how much they were suffering. I think we all were being pushed to financial fears, physical limits, and most of all, psychological cliff edges.

I was meditating every day, water fasting, and I managed to write and Self-publish *The Quarantine Handbook* in just eleven days. All in all I was basking in the cane-field countryside of Barbados and didn't really have a complaint in the world. I got quality time with my father for the first time since his kidney transplant. I got time with the new metallic stallion of a dog, Hugo, who—still in his puppy years—could be mistaken for a rideable animal with his noteworthy height. I got time with the fresh breeze and empathic sunshine and took in the sound of the cockatoo barking "kiss kiss."

Then, lockdown ended.

Society trickled back to functionality, and I wanted to execute on my vision. No one had time to listen. Honestly no one even really grasped my genius idea to innovate how we perceive and experience intelligence. I was adamant that I could liberate the intellect and enhance the efficacy of the everyday human. Perhaps I was and still am ahead of my time. Perhaps people were just scrambling to survive and had zero fucks to give about anything other than keeping their heads above turbulent waters. Fewer people around me were thriving and more were moving from struggling to suffering, and it was the wrong time to acquaint them with my ambitions.

Then I became one of them.

I became the first-place winner of suffering. It's called being suicidal. It was not my first rodeo, so I knew the difference between a bad day and never wanting to live another one. I remember the pain I felt to be living—living as my Self and feeling transparent, as if people looked straight through me.

I did it with such grace, so quietly, so hidden so as not to interrupt the busy souls.

Until I didn't.

I screamed, I cried, I deciphered the engineering of blades glued into shaving razors.

I chipped away at anything I had left in me that was thriving. I let my emotions bleed out until I felt nothing. At least when I felt nothing I didn't host the disappointment of being unloved, unseen, and unheard.

It is so much better to feel nothing at all, than to suffer in pain.

I spent longer hours in bed, slept more, felt emotionally heavier and heavier as days came and went. I skipped workouts and traded reading for Netflix, which just became background noise. I stopped using social media and didn't invest in my relationships, because what did I matter to anyone anyway? Everyone has their plate full; don't ask them to eat your shit.

I had a pity party, invited every destructive thought I could guest-list, and right there in the dark, we raved.

We raved like we wanted to die.

It was hauntingly dark. Without connection I wilted in the loneliness of being this created version of Self that I hated, and I assumed the world hated. I grew to believe it. I thought it was all true. Even in a room full of family, I didn't feel important, valid, worthy of anyone's attention because I felt ignored.

I am a genius, see me, hear me, believe in me. I craved that support and without it, the light went out. A glorious failure with a vision so mighty it would bring Goliath to his knees.

So we raved in the darkness. We raved like it would take days to slow us. Sweating in Self-loathing I laid in the fetal position and barfed at the thought of hosting my demons with such hospitality the way I had been. Get out, but stay. You are the only ones talking to me. In my quiet studio apartment, I needed silence from the thunder of my internal demolition.

My dad was so good at seeing me in all my glorious potential, so when I left the countryside to set up my little studio apartment, I was left with my Self.

I am not really sure why it cut so deep. Feeling invisible I guess made me feel worthless.

The only way out was in. I had to take control, and while I knew I couldn't be fake about what I was feeling, I thought maybe I could do things that would make me feel better. Rather than try to get rid of the crushing thoughts that pinned me down, I used my little might and tried to adjust my focus. I understood that taking action would create a biological sense of happiness simply by releasing happy chemicals. So I focused on my body instead of my mind.

Let Me Layman It for You

The body responds to instructions from the brain and the brain listens to the mind. If my mind was compromised, perhaps I could just get my body to take the action without the motivation of the mind. Maybe I just had to give up on feeling good before taking action.

If I could just work out, then my body would feel good because of the biological response to that action. That was the hardest part, because you don't feel like doing anything. I knew all the things I was meant to do, but there just seemed to be this huge barrier between where I got lost and taking one step in front of me to find relief.

I felt like getting in a ring with my demons, obliterating them for the pain they had inflicted, so I acted as if this workout was liberation.

It was a fight for freedom.

I've never been one to opt for medication. I didn't want that for myself, especially since reading in various articles that up to 50 percent of people on antidepressants receive little or no benefit. This was most recently documented in "An Overview of Treatment-Resistant Depression" published by VeryWellMind.com in November 2020, written by editor in chief Amy Morin, who is an author and psychotherapist. The article was reviewed by Steven Gans, who's served as a Clinical Challenge editor for the Harvard Review of Psychiatry and teaches at Massachusetts General Hospital. To me, those were not the most encouraging stats to push chemicals into my body, but that was just my personal decision, and each to their own. I know that studies are now looking at if people being prescribed antidepressants are actually even depressed. That might not be the case, and it's an even more encouraging reason for me to keep digging into the Self, esteem, and other factors that impact mood.

It did get me to thinking if meds were used for brain disorders, and I felt like my depression was actually emotionally rooted symptoms and nonclinical, then I could figure this out. I just needed to get from A to B and realized it had everything to do with the interconnectedness of the mind, brain, and body.

As we saw in the last chapter, some causes of depression stem from unresolved emotional trauma, Self-defeating mental habits, or lack of life vision and purpose. This could be why almost half the people on medication will not be relieved of their depression, because they need to figure out what's happening in their mind and with their Self.

Research by Julia Friederike Sowislo and Ulrich Orth (2013) explored if low Self-esteem predicted depression and anxiety. Their conclusion was that to protect your mood, you should focus on boosting Self-esteem. This supported my belief that low Self-esteem is a high-risk factor for depression, and that seemed like a great place to focus. I was encouraged by the extensive longitudinal studies published in Cambridge University Press that aimed to treat depressive symptoms with cognitive behavioral group therapy that focused on enhancing Self-esteem.

Self-esteem is normally determined at a young age. If you develop a certain low level as a child and never rectify it, it stays stable in that place. I assume it leads to a predisposition to depression. I was bullied as a kid. I was smart, but inside I can't say I was confident, loved, or even liked. I guess this episode of depression was a reflection of that inner child and her unresolved trauma.

Reckoning and Rewards

The thing is that our happiness is tuned to the body's reward system, which controls incentive, salience, motivation, and desire. Depression, I discovered, is also related to this reward system, and it's sort of like a glitch in your motivation and willingness to use energy and effort to experience a reward—an utter loss of interest.

The part of the brain that deals with motor and reward (the ventral striatum) is connected to the area of the brain that deals with Self-knowledge (the medial prefrontal cortex) and that connection (via a frontostriatal circuit) is related to Self-esteem. Our Self-esteem, Self-knowledge, and our state of desire, satisfaction, and happiness are interconnected.

As I burrowed further down my rabbit hole, the complexity of depression, much like a Japanese single malt, profoundly distilled itself into something remarkable. I started to see this big scary topic condense into a powerful theory. The concept of Self, the Affective Self, and Self-esteem were the core to healing depression.

Researchers Jamie L. Hanson, Annchen R. Knodt, Bartholomew D. Brigidi, and Ahmad R. Hariri published an article in Cambridge University Press (2017) titled "Heightened connectivity between the ventral striatum and medial prefrontal cortex as a biomarker for stress-related psychopathology: understanding interactive effects of early and more recent stress." This looked at the novel biomarkers linking stress in this specific part of the brain connections and depression.

The ventral striatum part of the brain is a critical component of the motor and reward system. Dysfunction in this part of the brain is often associated with both psychiatric and neurological disorders including obsessive-compulsive disorder, addiction, schizophrenia, Parkinson's disease, and Huntington's disease.

I truly believe that a person's level of Self-esteem impacts this particular brain connectivity, and understanding this relationship could treat depression, eating disorders, anxiety, and other mental illnesses. Understanding the brain's neuroscience and functioning allows us to better understand what drives our Self-concept, desires, thinking patterns, and actions, both happy and unhappy. It helps us to close the gap between ideals, desires, expectations, and the outcomes of behavior, satisfaction, and experience.

THE NEUROSCIENCE
OF HAPPINESS

Focus is often on the mind and its psychology when you think of depression and happiness, but your brain plays a major role in the neuroscience of happiness. Centuries have come and gone, and the human species has evolved in fascinating ways, especially when it comes to your skull, brain tissue, and the odd 100 billion neurons that make up your complex control center.

We have spoken about the reptilian brain, which is the lower region of the brain, as the most primal and least developed. It is where your survival instincts stem from. Human consciousness then developed in tandem with the brain. The upper brain, or the mammalian brain, provided us the lobes of the neocortex and reasoning brain comprising the frontal, the parietal, the temporal, and occipital lobes. The most developed states of our consciousness allow intelligence reasoning, emotional and thought analysis, and decision-making.

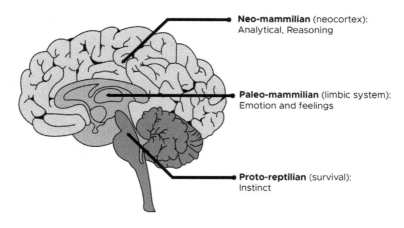

Diagram 4.1

Progressing from 1) its reptilian system focused on instinct to include 2) its limbic system centered on emotions and expanding to 3) the neocortex focused on thinking and reasoning. The brain has been quite the badass in what it has brought to our ability to experience life in more complex ways. This is the evolution from the Affective Self to the Cognitive Self and Executive Self. The mind, which deals with our psychology, meets with the brain's neurology in the prefrontal cortex at the front of the neocortex and transmits signals to our body in response to our reasoning. It allows Self-awareness and reflection, and it processes emotions through the limbic system to create understanding and make calculated behavioral decisions for the Executive Self.

Our metacognition is an executive ability that allows us to think about our own thinking, and it is possible because of our brain's incredible frontal lobe. It is in this brain region that we activate our decision-making. When faced with uncertainty and limited feedback, our metacognition will deliberate various scenarios, accuracy, likelihood, and predictability. This computational nature of thinking and deciphering what is good or bad comes from this brain segment, which equips us with the skill to problem solve and approach life strategically and mindfully. It helps us feel in control, and we like that.

Our perceptual expectancy of situations, paired with optimism, doesn't just ensure constructive metacognition. It also enhances performance outcomes. Executive functions like being able to process conflict, predict outcomes, curate expectations, and set goals are all related to this part of the brain. Imagine you lost these skills. I, for one, would spin out a whole lot more.

What started to fascinate me most about the prefrontal cortex was looking at how active it was in happy versus sad people. Studies hinted at it being the most active in happy people. Of particular interest was something I read in The World Happiness Report (2015), edited by John Helliwell, Richard Layard, and Jeffrey Sachs. In the summary of Chapter 5:The Neuroscience of Happiness, they wrote, "The prefrontal cortex and ventral striatum are especially important in sustained positive emotion." Of course, my next thoughts were how do we stimulate the prefrontal cortex, and could it be an opportunity to increase happiness from a neurological level? If we decreased the activities that stimulate the right prefrontal cortex, could we avoid sadness, despair, and potentially depression?

> *"The care of human life and happiness . . . is the*
> *only legitimate object of good government."*
> —THOMAS JEFFERSON (1809)

Positive thoughts, positive thinking about your thinking, positivity all around is related to our performance, happiness, life satisfaction, and well-being. Some scientifically proven techniques that aid in stimulating happiness in the brain include meditation, gratitude, affirmations, kindness, journaling, exercise, and optimism.

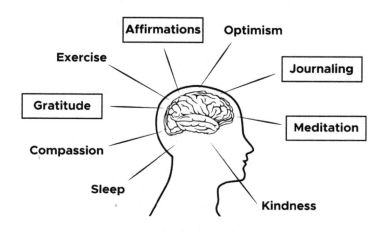

Diagram 4.2

Alongside the ways in which the prefrontal cortex supports our Cognitive and Executive functions, it also plays a large role in stress, anxiety, and sadness.

We learned that the brain's plasticity will create dominant neural pathways subject to what we repeat most consistently. Start to think about that in the context of emotional equilibrium, which is our set point of happiness and the awareness of our hedonic adaptation. As we condition the state of our emotions alongside our thoughts and beliefs, our brain's neural plasticity will naturally wire itself to the default set point of happiness, regardless of if it's negative or positive. I think if we tend to be dispositionally happy, we would endeavor to adopt positive thinking and reasoning. Our positive psychology actually aids the brain in producing happy hormones and neurotransmitters simply by conditioning our emotional Affective Self and thinking Cognitive Self to perceive things in ways that leave us feeling optimistic.

Changing our thoughts and beliefs can change our feelings. The brain responds to those feelings accordingly. Negative thoughts make it difficult to solve problems and inhibit creativity as well, as it slows the brain's coordination abilities. Fear will activate the survival instinct and thereby affect impulse control, mood, and even memory. I think the negativity and pessimism biases can actually impact our brain through our thinking.

Make an effort to be Self-aware so that you can improve cognition, productivity, attention, and focus.

Positivity is not just a trend, it's a superpower.

It actually significantly increases the synapses that connect neurons and allows them to communicate more effectively, solve problems more quickly, and enhance the mind's creative capacity. When you are expanding that positive plasticity, you are also able to think and analyze more efficiently and effectively. You become clearer, sharper, and more intuitive as you make sense of situations more quickly and with more ease and flow. The prefrontal cortex under the evaluation of positivity has found people are happier. They have healthier neural activity in the frontostriatal circuits. These circuits and communication channels are imperative for mediating motor, cognitive, and behavioral functions, leading to an enhanced relationship among the three Selves. This means that your positivity is improving your cognitive and behavioral interconnectedness. Your mind drives your actions. When these circuits are compromised, however, there is a potential for neurodegenerative disorders, such as Alzheimer's disease, Parkinson's disease, schizophrenia, depression, obsessive-compulsive disorder (OCD), and attention-deficit hyperactivity disorder (ADHD).

The amazing thing is that the brain wants you to experience pleasure and is designed to reinforce obtaining it through its reward system. It will reinforce the synapses and neural pathways in the prefrontal cortex that produce pleasure. Understanding how to manage pleasure to obtain happiness means you can exercise neuropsychological techniques to help you bridge the gap.

There is, however, a significant difference between pleasure and happiness that we should look at.

THE PAIN OF PLEASURE

Happiness is a state that can either be hedonic or eudaimonic. We can experience happiness through instant gratification or delayed gratification. On the other hand, there are things that bring us pleasure in the moment versus satisfaction in the long term. It's good for us to grasp happiness as a state of mind that is internally motivated while understanding that pleasure is externally motivated and can be a reaction to stimuli.

Happiness could be the perception we have as we apply our thinking toward external stimuli and choose a feeling in response to our environment and situations. This is internal and requires the Affective and Cognitive Selves to feel first and then reflect. It is really important that we choose the perspective that leaves us happy. This type of reflection is a part of metacognition, and it starts with Self-awareness.

Happiness is more long-lived than momentary pleasure.

We can feel happy about life even though we may have had a disheartening experience, simply by putting the experience into perspective and engaging in appreciation. This is how Self-awareness can result in chosen gratification. By practicing mindfulness, we can enhance states of happiness by focusing on the now instead of our past encounters of pain. When there is alignment among our feelings, beliefs, and behavior, there is a closing of the gap, and we feel happy.

Pleasure is a feeling of enjoyment, dependent on external factors and usually momentary in nature. So should we be chasing pleasure, happiness, or both?

Addictive Pleasure vs Authentic Happiness

Dopamine
Pleasure

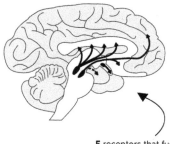

5 receptors that fuel
desire and motivation

Serotonin
Happiness

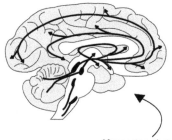

14 receptors that
fuel happiness

Dopamine	Serotonin
a) Temporary feeling in the body, visceral	a) Lasting feeling in the mind, ethereal
b) Addictive	b) Not addictive
c) Desires more	c) Feels enough
d) Related to gambling, excessive narcotics, smoking, binge eating, and shopping	d) Related to healthy relationships, career, and community
e) Drives taking from others	e) Drives giving to others
f) Too much is destructive: addiction	f) Too little is destructive: depression

Diagram 4.3: Brueck, H. & Lee, S. (2018, March 24).
This is why our phones are making us miserable: happiness isn't the same thing as
pleasure, and our brain knows it. *Business Insider.*
https://www.businessinsider.com/why-our-phones-are-making-us
-miserable-pleasure-isnt-happiness-2018-3.

There is a risk when we mistake pleasure for happiness.

It can lead to addiction or feeling dependent on those external factors for what we might think is happiness. With pleasure, the brain will
release a chemical called dopamine, a neurotransmitter and one of
the most dominant of the happy hormones, also known as the reward

molecule. There is a relationship between this and the brain's other neurotransmitters, such as serotonin, commonly known as the confidence molecule. Low levels of serotonin have long been thought to put people at risk of depression and can lead to overproduction of dopamine, which enhances impulsive behavior. Our impulses or lack of motivation are related to our level of neurotransmitters.

Serotonin influences mood, memory, appetite, metabolism, and digestion, but more importantly, increased serotonin levels have been shown to improve the overall mood of a person and aid in treating depression. Imagine when our serotonin dips, our mood mirrors that and we are left feeling depressed. People who turn to sources of pleasure that are unsustainable, for instance use of narcotics, will often have mood swings as their dopamine and serotonin levels spike and plummet.

The other thing about pleasure and dopamine is that repetition of activity in the pleasure center of the brain will create a loss of those dopamine receptors that makes the feeling of pleasure so sensational. We grow accustomed to the sensation of pleasure, we build tolerance, and we end up needing more of the same thing to feel the exact same level of pleasure.

This is what results in addiction and why prioritizing pleasure and calling it happiness is destructive to well-being. Substance abuse and excessive consumption stems from all types of pleasure sources. That includes anything from sugar to alcohol, digital media, cocaine, or uncontrollable gambling. Do not be fooled. Things we think are not a problem could be synthetic happiness. Those shopping sprees, binge-eating benders, or endless one-night stands are all up for consideration when it comes to conscious choice of pleasure.

I'm not throwing any stones as a person who lived in the glass house of numbing pleasures, but I am saying we can all benefit from learning the difference.

The Skin I'm In

Pleasure is an area of research that has been studied since the 1930s when psychologist B.F. Skinner created the Skinner Box, an operant conditioning chamber with a lever press for food and water reward, and a lever for punishment via painful shock. Rats repeatedly pressed the reward lever and avoided the punishment lever. This aligns with the work by Freud and Maslow, which indicates that humans are stimulated and motivated by pleasure and an ability to Self-actualize.

As we covered earlier, the default is that we seek pleasure and avoid pain, and thereby our survival will prioritize the avoidance of pain over the seeking of pleasure. However, when there is no threat, we will sometimes irrationally pursue pleasure.

By the 1950s, Skinner's work continued, and psychologists James Olds and Peter Milner modified the chamber to deliver direct brain stimulation via deeply implanted electrodes. The research proved incredibly insightful and shifted the entire field of behavioral neuroscience.

Rats pressed the lever up to 7,000 times per hour to stimulate their brain's pleasure center with the reward stimulation.

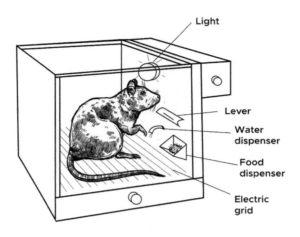

Diagram 4.4

Even when given the choice between pleasure and food when hungry, or water when thirsty, the rats would still prefer the pleasure stimulation circuit. Male rats ignored females, female rats abandoned their nursing newborns, and the only thing that mattered was hitting the lever of stimulation that gave them pleasure. It was remarkable that they were choosing it up to 2,000 times per hour for twenty-four hours in the face of other choices, even when faced with very critical survival needs. Some rats made this choice up until its likely deadly end.

The researchers needed to end their participation in the experiment to prevent death by starvation.

This experiment was then conducted on a human patient named B-19 and yielded similar findings. Understandably, due to ethical compliance, large human studies were avoided. Regardless, for me it was a shocking discovery (*excuse the pun*). I read the research, now questioning just how powerful the pursuit of pleasure can be, and how it operates sometimes to the detriment of even our survival instinct,

The Intelligence of Happiness

basic needs, rational thinking, and reasoning. I think the brain's reward center is critical to get in check if people are to have a fighting chance at happiness.

When you are eliminating bad habits, make sure you understand what kind of pleasure connection you had to the bad habit. Then do a strategic substitution and elect an alternative behavior that stimulates rewards. Suggestions include: meditation, journaling, gratitude, sports, drinking water, repeating an affirmation mantra, surrounding yourself with people who hold you accountable, positive reinforcement of good habits, supportive empowering Self-talk, orgasms, dancing, prayer, hypnosis, and charity work. We get into this deeper in the next and final chapter, which covers the techniques for bridging the gap.

Identify a bad habit and strategically substitute it for one of the above recommendations and then repeat, repeat, repeat the healthier habit.

The brain's neuroplasticity responds well to this kind of consistency and repetition. Neurons that fire together will wire together, and once they do, the hard becomes easy.

The only way to remove resistance is action.

The hard thing is to actually break bad habits, but the repetition of new habits will be simulated and supported by the brain as it reinforces anything that brings pleasurable rewards. We just need to remember that we cannot simply remove bad habits without substituting for something that also delivers rewards. Withdrawals and a lot of uneasy emotions will ensue. Be warned.

We need to ensure we are tapping into all of the brain's positive neurotransmitters and the body's happy hormones. That alignment will support a successful transformation.

NEUROPSYCHOLOGICAL
ALIGNMENT

When it comes to your happiness, you have options. Your psychology and the way thoughts and emotions can influence your behavior is only one spectrum of consideration. We can also look at the biological process of how the body's behavior affects thoughts and feelings. That, too, can drive happiness. There is a bidirectional route as to how we can obtain our joy, pleasure, happiness, and ultimate life satisfaction.

Neuroscientists will focus more on the biology of the brain and functionality of the nervous system, while psychologists use their research to better understand the mind and how it drives human behavior.

The brain is an organ that has a physical form and matter that weighs approximately 3.3 pounds, equating to 2 percent of your body weight. It is approximately 75 percent water, which means dehydration likely will have a negative impact on brain functioning. Your brain health matters for your happiness. The biochemical and cellular balance of the brain is disrupted in ways that impact physiology and even hormone balance, which directly impacts your happiness. Around 20 percent of the body's oxygen and blood supply are used by the brain, which takes up a substantial portion of your energetic resources.

You need to manage your brain to manage your energy.

How energized you feel impacts motivation and Self-efficacy. Therefore, it influences the Executive Self and behavior. If you do not address the brain, then working on the psychology of the mind alone can prove to be ineffective.

The word neuropsychology sounds intimidating. We write it off as some type of overly academic or scientific field reserved for highly qualified doctors, but when we break it down, we start to see how everything we learned to this point is packaged as a whole under this field of science. To look at mental health holistically, I felt that there were ways in which the brain and its neurology could impact depression and happiness alike that could complement the traditional approach of the mind and psychology.

Neurology will cover most biological and nervous systems interactions, such as ways in which hormones and neurotransmitters influence mood, motivation, reward, love, happiness, and many other outcomes that relate to the body's state of chemical balance.

While we may experience temporary pleasure, hedonic and transient happiness comes with instant gratification, and with the dopamine flowing, we feel a reward that is short-lasting and addictive. Ideally we want to be able to leverage our three Selves to work with the brain's healthiest level of hormones and neurotransmitters.

The three main focus points that have helped me are grouped as follows:

- **The Brain**—the nervous system and neurotransmitters
- **The Mind**—psychology, thoughts, and emotions
- **The Body**—the endocrine system and hormones

The difference between neurotransmitters and hormones is that they are different types of chemical signals. They are produced and active in different parts of the body. The nervous system produces your neurotransmitters, and the endocrine system produces hormones. Let's review a bit about each of these before we move on to how they will influence your happiness through thoughts, motivation, and even concentration.

Excited yet?

The Brain, Nervous System,
and Neurotransmitters

There are these awesome chemical messengers that carry the signals among the nerve cells in our body: our neurotransmitters. They are deployed specifically to other neurons, glands, and muscles and instruct the body's automatic functions like our heart beating, breathing, and physiological regulation. Billions of them keep us able to dominate life, that is, if they are properly balanced.

The impact of neurotransmitters is short-lived and affects both our voluntary and involuntary actions. We make choices around our behavior and actions, for instance what we consume or leisure activities we prefer, and these chemicals have an influence on how those choices are made. Neurotransmitters have a very local and fast-acting impact and facilitate the signals between neurons in the brain. They influence our mood, memory, sleep patterns, sex drive and appetite, and they are large dictators of what we may form addictions to.

The main neurotransmitters related to mental health, happiness, and well-being are dopamine, serotonin, endorphins, oxytocin, GABA, and norepinephrine. Let's dip our toe into each one of these molecule pools, shall we?

Dopamine: The Pleasure Hormone or Reward Molecule

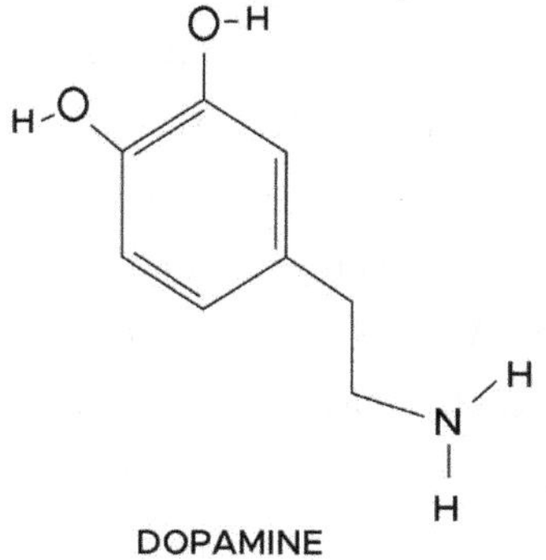

DOPAMINE
Pleasure

Diagram 4.5

One of the most important of all neurotransmitters is dopamine, which focuses on reward-driven behavior and how we seek pleasure. Settings goals, motivations, and desires, accomplishing them, and satisfying objectives releases dopamine. We obtain pleasure from the release of dopamine, especially when we have done a good job and meet our own expectations. This rush of joy becomes addictive and we can get it from the wrong places, like satisfying food cravings from junk, nicotine in cigarettes, alcoholic drinking, gambling, sex, and drugs.

The question is not what gives us pleasure, but if how we get our pleasure leaves us happy.

If we only experience momentary and temporary pleasure, then we start to turn to those sources for the next dopamine hit. It's a destructive continuum of fleeting feelings. The problem is that the body's threshold changes, meaning we need more to get the same dopamine high. It's that tolerance we touched on earlier.

Stay away from reliance on that type of synthetic happiness.

Get off the slippery slope.

Unnatural inducers of dopamine also impact the body's natural ability to produce this neurotransmitter. This means when we withdraw from artificial means of pleasure, the body is not producing it as it regularly should, and we feel what some might call a comedown or emotional low. We have changed our emotional equilibrium and set point of happiness. We have to be ready to manage this part of change as we substitute naughty pleasures for healthy ones.

Beyond dopamine's feel-good properties, it impacts motor skills, movement, attention, learning, and mood. When we lose our dopamine neurons, the body could develop degenerative diseases like Parkinson's disease. Low levels of dopamine will result in a lack of motivation, memory loss, mood swings, fatigue, and even depression. If we rely on the wrong sources for dopamine, then we could develop dangerously addictive behavior just to avoid these low emotions and the symptoms of declining dopamine. Even when dopamine was deficient in lab mice, they refused to eat because they lacked the motivation to do so. Even when food was available, the mice would choose to starve if they did not have dopamine. Their motivations changed and their ability to concentrate on anything outside of their pleasure was impacted.

Dopamine from the right behaviors actually assists the brain to optimize your intelligence. It enhances our Executive Self's ability to plan, set goals, and even navigate complex communication and social interaction. All three Selves—our emotions and felt Affective Self, our ability to think and our known Cognitive Self, and the motivation of our active Executive Self—are impacted by dopamine.

The reality is that if we have no pleasure, we easily lack happiness. We have to understand the right ways to obtain pleasure that are not reliant on disruptive dopamine production and addiction to destructive consumption patterns and behaviors.

When we work with the body's natural biology, dopamine is produced in doses that are super beneficial for joy, wakefulness, coordination, productivity, and goal achievement. Some natural sources for dopamine include a diet that contains the l-tyrosine amino acid, which dopamine is made from. Choosing a protein-rich diet that contains lots of these dopamine-enriching foods includes apples, beets, watermelon, bananas, avocados, green leafy vegetables, oregano, and turmeric. You ideally want to reduce your intake of saturated fats, introduce healthy probiotics into your diet, and get plenty of rest and exposure to sunlight.

Additionally, get moving.

Exercise is a great way to improve the flow of nutrients to the brain, and it increases our levels of dopamine, serotonin, and norepinephrine. My personal favorite is meditation, daily. It has benefits that far outweigh just healthy dopamine production, and we cover that more later.

Serotonin: The Happy Hormone or Confidence Molecule

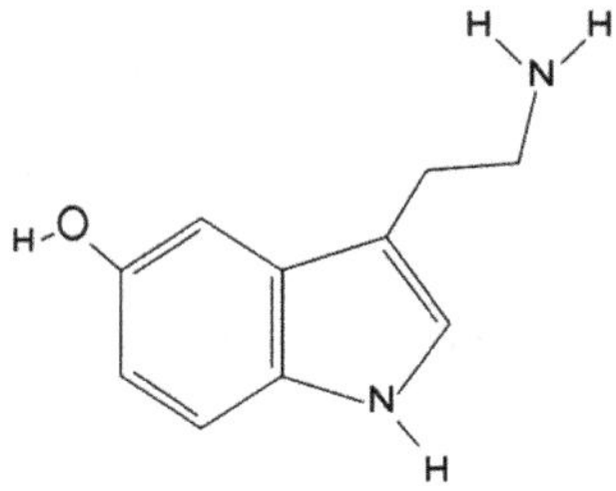

SEROTONIN
Happiness

Diagram 4.6

While dopamine largely influences motivation, serotonin influences confidence and social behavior. Also, like dopamine, it regulates mood and sleep. Serotonin also relieves pain and aids to enhance Self-esteem and our feeling of worthiness, which will assist in improving the state of our Affective Self. With high Self-esteem, we reduce the risk of depression and create more opportunities to find happiness as we feel a sense of belonging. As we move higher up the hierarchy of needs, we strive for Self-actualization, eudaimonic happiness, and a life of purpose and meaning.

While dopamine also is released with accomplishment, increasing serotonin levels reinforces the sense of accomplishment. Serotonin levels can decrease when we are having unnaturally high levels of dopamine, which can leave us feeling depressed. This is why most antidepressant and antianxiety medications focus on balancing serotonin levels. When these levels are not balanced, we actually also experience brain fog, sleeplessness, and even paranoia, especially if levels are unnaturally spiking and dipping. I believe this is associated with a synthetic means of happiness and addictive pleasures.

To keep this happiness chemical in check, get some bright light exposure through time in the sun. You can also integrate exercise into your lifestyle and even visualization techniques that focus on happy moments and recalling positive memories. All of these simple tips will provide serotonin.

Happy memories aren't good only for serotonin, but also for endorphins.

Endorphins: The Relief Hormone or Pain-Stopping Molecule

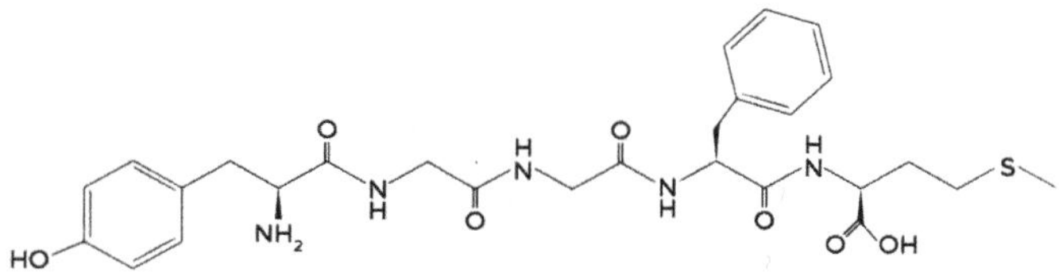

ENDORPHIN
Pain Relief

Diagram 4.7

Known for their pain-killing qualities, endorphins are some of the most powerful neurotransmitters. If they are low, we experience greater levels of physical and emotional pain and anxiety, and are at greater risk of feeling depressed. To help the body deal with physical pain, these epic opioid neuropeptides are like our very own Self-produced morphine. Anyone who has ever had severe pain can celebrate this amazing chemical.

The central nervous system and particularly our brain's pituitary gland will produce these chemicals from exercise, which results in that post-workout high you love, much like runner's high but also obtainable from something as simple as thirty minutes of walking. Don't be mistaken: you do not have to get on the CrossFit Insanity workout train to get this high. You can get it from time in nature, laughter, human connection, orgasms, and acupuncture. There are many options that promote feelings of euphoria when we stimulate our endorphin production.

Oxytocin: The Love Hormone or Bonding Molecule

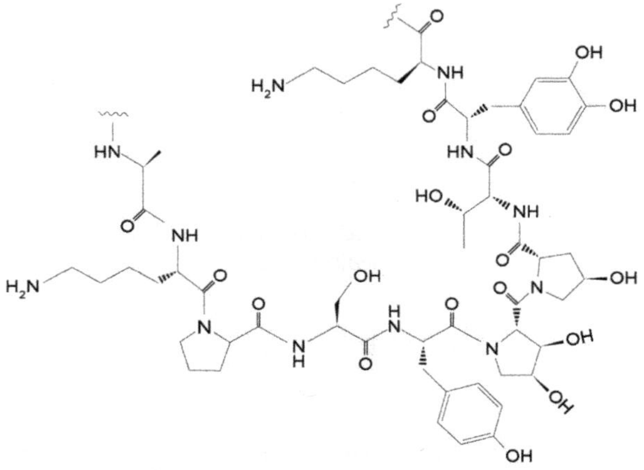

OXYTOCIN
Love

Diagram 4.8

This neurotransmitter helps us with social recognition and bonding, especially when it comes to trust and loyalty. There have been correlations between oxytocin and romantic attachment as well as sexual reproduction. It is the reason new mothers are so attached to their children during pregnancy and breastfeeding.' It's also what gives that high with the drug MDMA, which leaves people loving, touchy, and in a state of what appears to be deep and meaningful bonding, at least in that particular moment. High levels of oxytocin equals your warm and fuzzy, friendly energy, but you do not need drugs to get this high.

We can simply show affection, love, cuddle, or pat an animal to increase our oxytocin levels. This love hormone is one that we can naturally stimulate through massage, yoga, listening to music, meditation, masturbation, kindness, petting animals, spending time with friends and family whose company we enjoy, having sex, and engaging in empathic behaviors. Love makes you feel good; it makes you feel relaxed.

GABA: The Relaxation Hormone or Anti-anxiety Molecule

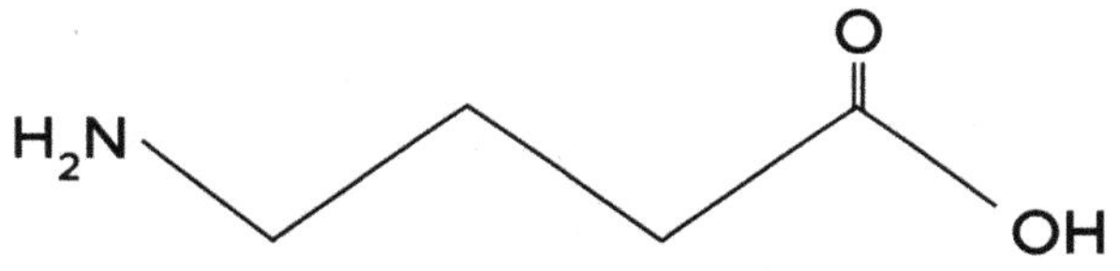

GABA
Relaxation

Diagram 4.9

This is the neurotransmitter responsible for feelings of relaxation and calm, and it is no surprise that the techniques mentioned time and again apply here, too. GABA slows your neurons frantically firing, so it allows a sense of calm to be felt. To increase GABA, reduce anxiety, and increase our happiness, take up yoga or meditation, practice more presence in the moment, and be mindful. Increased levels of this neurotransmitter will aid in improving your sleep, and research continues to explore its relationship with disease prevention for diabetes, cardiovascular disease, and cancer. It is believed to be antioxidant, anti-inflammatory, and antimicrobial. Keep an eye on this one.

Norepinephrine: The Stress Hormone or Fight-or-Flight Molecule

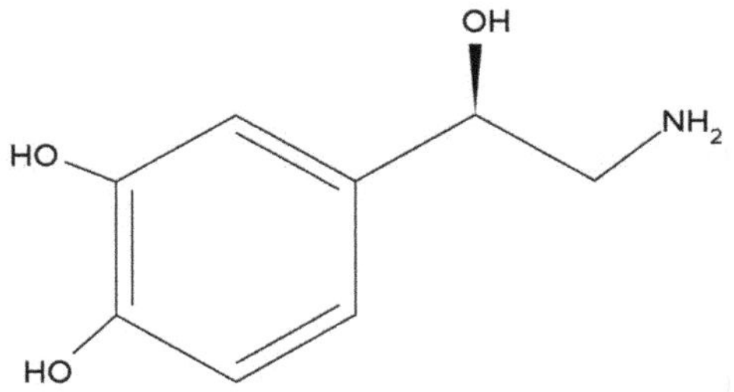

NOREPHRINE
Stress

Diagram 4.10

Aside from our relaxation neurotransmitter, we need to address our stress neurotransmitter, norepinephrine. This is the chemical responsible for the body's fight-or-flight response and is very much linked to our Affective Self through emotions like fear and anger. It's the one that keeps us in survival mode instead of soaring toward Self-actualization, so we want to make sure it's in check. If we are always focused on avoiding pain, we will not be pursuant of pleasure. Our stress neurotransmitter is an inhibitor to our happiness and when produced, it can trigger anxiety and depression, and will mess with our motivation. We can balance this neurotransmitter through good sleep, exercise, small accomplishments, and meditation.

Now that we understand a bit about the brain, nervous system, and our amazing neurotransmitters, here is some further insight as to the recommended actions that were touched on for healthy brain balance and things that improve the state of our mind and body.

Meditation. This strengthens our ability to regulate emotions and the stability of our mood. It will seriously help with constructive responsiveness to life rather than reactivity to life in ways that are destructive. This simple exercise integrating long inhales and exhales is one of the most powerful actions we can take for inner peace, ease, and the feeling of lightness. Focus on your breath, inhales, and exhales. Focus on the awareness of your thoughts as you objectively allow them to pass like clouds moving in the sky, in and out of your mind. The more you practice meditation, like with exercise, the more you will notice the benefits. Meditation enhances our behavioral regulation and impulse control. Alongside that, meditation will help our attention become more focused, improving our ability to perceive and put things in perspective and to feel in life's divine flow. This gem of a technique will induce our body's relaxation response, leaving us clear-minded, calm, and able to make better decisions. Meditation is a way that you can use the mind to change the brain and benefit the body.

Gratitude. Something as simple as writing down a list of daily blessings or utilizing reminders to notify you throughout the day to think of something that you are grateful for will help you tune into appreciation mode. This can significantly improve the reward system and the body's release of both serotonin and dopamine. That means doses of happiness and pleasure leaving you basking in rewards. Even if this is reflective and we recall happy memories, such action will also produce serotonin and leave us feeling happy in our present moment. I get it every time I go through my favorite album and think about how grateful I am to have made so many meaningful memories in my life. I am so grateful for the people I was able to experience life with and the places I explored all over the world. Expressing gratitude and being thankful toward our friends, family, and colleagues also leaves us feeling positive. I have my alarms set as the name "gratitude," my iCal reminders, notes on my wall, and any trick I can use to stay conscious of this all-powerful state throughout the day.

Physical activity. Exercise, even light to moderate, produces levels of serotonin that lower hostility and decrease the symptoms of depression. As little as a five-minute walk outside in natural light increases motivation, improves Self-esteem, and improves overall mood. Exercise also releases endorphins, which relieve pain, and increases norepinephrine to combat stress and provide more motivation. Moving is magic.

Sunlight. Natural light exposure correlates with increases in both serotonin and dopamine levels, which improves the symptoms of depression, but even if you are not depressed, it will still act as a mood enhancer. Get into the delicious sunshine, get the serotonin levels up, and get that satisfaction of happiness.

Coffee. Consuming coffee, which I absolutely adore, actually allows the brain to block the reabsorption of dopamine. It slows the rate at which it leaves the brain, leaving us feeling that pleasure and reward sensation longer. This also makes caffeine addictive, so be sure to monitor consumption and sometimes withdraw so you can continue to savor the reward feeling before the body requires more of it to get the same stimulation. In light of the good, old, hedonic adaptation, turn to abstinence to reinstate savoring.

Essential plant oils. The smell of lavender and lemon have both been found to increase the release of dopamine and serotonin in the brain. Lavender in particular is known for its calming effect, as are many other essential oils that have become popular in aromatherapy to overcome anxiety and insomnia.

Now Help Me Take Action

It's fine to tell you what works, but how can you feel motivated to perform these actions?

I believe that has to be a critical priority point. Knowledge without action is useless. While I am highly motivated, live by these techniques, and have felt firsthand the massive ways in which they have been beneficial for my life, there was a conditioning time frame when keeping up with them was a daunting struggle. After all, depression inhibits the motivation or interest in anything.

We have to condition our Cognitive Self to support the behavioral element of Self, and simply take action because that action is what will tip us into the chemical states that shift motivation.

We have to be willing to get our Self to do it.

Without doing, there will be no results, no relief, and no rewards.

When you do not know how to stop the mental noise that is negative in nature, burdensome, and haunting, focus on putting your shoes on and just get moving out the door. Breathing deeply might be the only thing you end up doing to shift heavy emotions, even when you do not know how to understand them. The work you do with your Affective Self focuses on identifying your emotions. Your Cognitive Self is embracing and understanding those emotions and choosing thoughts about them that lead to healthier feelings and perceptions. Your Executive Self is actively doing things that support getting from where you are to where you want to be emotionally, mentally, and physically.

Action is necessary, and if you focus on changing behavior, that is a winning bet.

When your mindset is compromised, you can shift your priority from your psychology to your neurological control center. Let your

Executive Self take action so the brain and its neurotransmitters aid you where your mind may struggle with emotions and thoughts.

I believe that we can close the Authenticity Gap of Happiness by taking our neuropsychology into account and deepening our understanding of the relationship between the brain and the mind. A fundamental area that I have found to influence our ability to be happy and obtain greater life satisfaction is neuroplasticity. It is our ability to adapt, adopt new responses, change, and grow.

Neuroplasticity

Don't panic, it's just another big word.

If you are open to it, you might actually find your relationship with your brain's plasticity quite intriguing. Plasticity is the brain's ability to change, grow, and rewire itself. The brain operates through communication via synaptic transmission, where one cell releases a neurotransmitter and the receiving cell absorbs, which is known as neuronal firing. The more frequently this communication happens over the same pathway, the easier and faster communication becomes, which essentially is the origin of the saying "neurons that fire together, wire together." The repetition of specific communication creates automation and you develop habits. We all know how much easier things are that have become habitual. This dominant wiring is what makes bad habits so hard to break, because those communication pathways that instruct behavior have become the autopilot for the mind and body.

The brain has the capability to empower you with learning new skills and adapting to changing environments, altering its entire form and functionality even as we age.

If we can change the things we repeat, we can change our entire Self-concept.

Our brain does this most easily through repetition of certain emotions, thoughts, beliefs, and behaviors. Whether or not this plasticity is beneficial depends completely on the nature of the emotions, thoughts, beliefs, and behaviors we are activating and whether they are constructive or destructive. If we are choosing destructive emotions consistently, or choosing to think in ways that create a Self-defeating mindset or behave in ways that reinforce bad habits, then we will develop a negative plasticity.

Negative Plasticity

Negative plasticity is degenerative for the brain, which means our negative feelings, perception, and worldview are depressive in how they impact our brain health. As you saw from both the negativity and pessimism biases, we default to those mindsets because they are most dominantly used. The more we sustain that negativity, the worse it is for our brain health and mental health.

Our brain develops in coherence with our points of focus, making it easier to revert to those patterns of thinking, emotional reactions, belief systems, and behaviors. Repetition creates habits and conditioning. If those habits are bad, then negative neuroplasticity will keep our Authenticity Gap of Happiness wide open. If not, help it to expand because it is much easier to follow a habitual routine. The pathways continuously used are the ones that are quicker to follow because they are known, familiar, and feel safe. Repetition creates our autopilot, our preferred existence, and our comfort zone. This becomes our default for any or all of our three Selves.

Humans have evolved in ways that prevent danger, seek comfort, and put safety and security as priorities, as we have seen with the survival instinct. One thing that has aided that is the negativity bias, because when things of equal intensity transpire, those things that are negative in nature will have a greater psychological effect than things which are neutral or even positive. That has kept our species safe.

Our preference is toward negativity, even when faced with something equally emotionally impactful, as we have touched on a few times now. Try to think about how your thoughts and behavior are triggered when something negative happens compared to the multitude of neutral or positive things that are always happening. We glorify the negative, the problematic, the challenging, the hurtful, and the destructive things in our life. We are consumed at times by this negativity bias, which through more dedicated energy becomes the stronger default pathway for the brain to choose when forming our emotions, perceptions, and feelings.

All of this impacts our behavior and life experience.

The negativity bias can actually influence our belief systems and how we form our expectations in life. Negative plasticity makes it difficult to shift Self-perception, because it is easy to remain in the place where your brain has created dominant neural pathways.

It then requires great effort to break negative ways, but I know we can and will succeed.

In our current world, focusing on the negative with an overwhelming amount of negative stimulus weighs extremely heavily on the brain. This type of cognition leaves one exhausted, emotionally compromised, and mentally ill. The more we repeat this lifestyle, the more instinctive and automated it will become as the brain forms neuronal connections based on what is repeated, regardless of if that repetition is forming healthy habits or destructive ones. The brain does not care; it will wire what you fire.

The Intelligence of Happiness

Proceed with caution, as your cognition is creating your conditioning.

In its most basic form, using the brain to worry about mundane dynamics of life will without a doubt become a signature trait of existence. What you condition will continue, even when you don't realize that it's happening automatically.

You will eventually sink and potentially drown in sadness.

Habits are hard to form, yet easy to maintain. This involves focusing on our neuroplasticity, and through intention and continuity, forming easy and Self-benefiting thoughts. It is our power to choose life-enhancing beliefs, constructive emotions, and beneficial behaviors.

Choose the positive; make this your dominant default.

Positive Plasticity

Positive neuroplasticity is a nurturing and enhanced focus on positive emotions and positive mindset. It helps the brain become more resilient and overcome injuries, learning disabilities, stroke, and mental illnesses like depression, addiction, ADD, ADHD, OCD, and even symptoms of autism by enhancing the healthy functioning of the brain. It correlates to mood, attention, and memory and allows the brain to be more efficient and organized, thereby reducing levels of anxiety and other symptoms of depression.

Developing positive plasticity allows us to feel more in control of aligning emotions, thoughts, beliefs, and behaviors. We can train our brain and mind through journaling and meditation to perception modes that induce happiness and naturally gravitate more toward joy, love, gratitude, compassion, and thereby higher Self-esteem and better life satisfaction.

This is done through the practices of optimism, gratitude, and hopefulness, which are all directly linked to our level of happiness. Using positive neuroplasticity to develop habits of delayed gratification helps establish eudaimonic happiness and long-term life satisfaction.

Positive plasticity helps close the gap.

So how do you develop positive plasticity?

It's easier than you think, but I won't mislead you—change is uncomfortable. Preparing yourself for change through an awareness of that discomfort creates an ability to withstand it. You have to perceive the context of your discomfort and understand that it is part of a bigger transformation.

A little bit of pain now for lasting happiness later.

Be gentle on your Self, be patient, be kind, positively affirm your efforts, and greet struggles with Self-love.

Remember the power of Self-compassion.

Minimize your social comparisons unless they instill motivation on your journey. Look up to those who inspire you. Stay tuned into things that fill you up and keep you focused.

The secret of successfully changing your Self is *consistency*.

What you repeat reaps what you become.

Condition yourself to value satisfaction more than sacrifice. Energy flows where your attention goes. If you are always thinking about what you are giving up, you will feel loss. Think about what you are getting in the end and you will feel gain.

The time and energy you will use is your sacrifice, the satisfaction is your happiness, your amazement in life, your improved performance, your prosperity, your ability to attract more opportunity, love, and abundance into your life.

Our beliefs are a critical driving force in this life-improvement plan. We have to believe in our Self, believe in the ability to really connect to high vibrational emotions constantly, feel deep appreciation for life, and feel energizing love from living it.

It is so crucial, and I cannot stress this enough, that you build a lifestyle and consistency around positive plasticity in your emotions, thoughts, beliefs, and behaviors. You will not immediately feel better because of the sporadic increase in these neurotransmitters, but through time, new pathways, nerves, and connections will form.

Put things in perspective. It is a few weeks of rewiring for a lifetime of living in better spirits.

Leverage your brain, your mind, and your body to enhance your well-being.

MIND, BRAIN, BODY CONNECTION

As we are now aware, at our most primal level, we are a species that feels through the Affective Self, where a stimuli and reaction or response is constantly being activated in the limbic system and processed through our reptilian or thinking brain.

With a more developed consciousness, we can navigate constructively from the Affective Self to the Cognitive Self where we reason and judge situations. Then we engage our Executive Self to conduct chosen behaviors. Our level of development in this state of consciousness will largely determine what behavior we lead with. Understanding the mind, brain, and body connection will aid you in aligning your emotions, thoughts, beliefs, and behaviors in ways that optimize your happiness and life.

The mind is observing and making sense of what the body is feeling. Sometimes if you hear a noise in the house, you instantly feel a heightened awareness. You might feel on edge, your heart starts racing a little, and maybe if you are like me, you break into a little sweat in the anticipation of a threat. It does not take a lot to rattle me and make me feel that looming-in-the-darkness horror movie vibe. The body will hear a sound stimulus, and the mind will analyze it.

Sometimes you lead with instinct and then intellect.

You release adrenaline, which now has your fight-or-flight hormone in full swing ready to save your life, and then you find out it's the wind. You calm down and realize that the feeling of fear was just instinct. Your Cognitive Self takes over, and your perception of threat subsides as your Executive Self goes to shut the window.

There are very real biological and neurological ways in which your body takes course, from which it now can return to emotional and hormonal equilibrium. This is a simple example of how the three Selves relate to the state of mind, brain, and body. The situation could have been different. If I really felt something was off, however, and thought that someone was trying to break in through the window, that perception of the situation would yet again change my biological and neurological activity. What we think, believe, and choose to do are all one interconnected system.

We can navigate what comes after stimuli; it might be reaction or it might be response.

If we know an action will create a biological reaction, then we could lead with the Executive Self to get a response in the Affective Self. For instance, I could have a belief that working out will make me feel good and that creates enhanced Self-efficacy where I am incentivized to work out. I believe in my capability to take the action to work out because I believe that act will result in the reward felt by my Affective Self. My positive biological responses, such as the release of dopamine or endorphins, as well as the psychological presence in the mind, will result in emotions of accomplishment, satisfaction, and pride. Just taking action when I actually have little to no energy, motivation, or interest, enables me to hack the mind-brain-body connection.

Sometimes you have to push to override the Cognitive Self—what you think you know or believe about your situation in that given moment. There will be instances when you do not feel like doing anything, and you need to put the Affective Self to the side and energize the Executive Self.

If we constantly stay in a loop of how we feel and what we think, we may never actually *do*. Energy flows where attention goes. We need to make sure we are choosing the right Self.

If you are an overthinker or procrastinator, you might want to prioritize the Executive Self and focus on action, behavior, and drive, rather than linger in the back-and-forth thought loop that adjusts your beliefs to validate staying in your comfort zone and putting off tasks just a little longer.

When it comes to happiness, if you feel stuck in your funk, you may want to get out for a walk, do a meditation, or try some mindfulness and gratitude exercises that steer your Self out of your Affective and Cognitive stagnation. Taking action will shift your lingering states as you introduce alternative stimuli in your life. Your innate intelligence perceives and activates other spectrums of mind and brain when exposed to new experiences.

If you feel guilt about something that happened and you cannot change it, you might linger over and over about that decision. With that focus stuck in your mind, you develop low Self-esteem, feel like a bad person, and could even question your Self-knowledge about who you are as a whole, rather than who you were during just that one incident. This is the ideal time to shift gears into Executive mode, during which the endorphins and dopamine will improve the states of Self-esteem from a chemical neurotransmitter level. Instead of approaching things from the psychological level, we can also approach them neurologically or biologically.

I know it is not this simple, but keeping it this simple has worked for me. I have focused on the ways in which my neurology and psychology will create responses to an action taken with my biology and physiology.

I value action just as much as, if not more than, I value mindset.

I know if I can get my body to move, it would produce the chemicals to provide the ups that my mind alone is unable to create. That's what neurotransmitters are there for. They make us feel anything from dopamine and the pleasure hormone, to oxytocin and the love hormone, to serotonin and the happiness hormone.

It is in the brain that we control our motivation-reward complex, so we need to include the brain if we want to have a well-rounded understanding of Self.

When you cannot get your mind right, know that your brain and your body have ways to support your happiness and well-being. This is the power of neuropsychology and the ways in which those three things—the mind, brain, and body—work together to impact our life.

Now let's get to the grand finale: bridging the gap.

BRIDGING
THE
GAP

---

*To live the rest of our life
as our Self, makes it the greatest
investment of our lifetime.*

I FOUND MYSELF REPEATING, "I AM NOTHING," AND those three words just brought me so much comfort. I am not sure if it was just the fact that I did not have to live up to any expectations of my Self if I was simply nothing. Simplistic and yet so colossal a statement.

I surrendered into nothingness.

It wasn't actually something that made me feel sad. I just felt that I placed less emphasis on everything I was trying to be and simply just *was*.

I am nothing.

I am nothing.

I am nothing.

And this statement flowed and evolved from my gentle, forgiving, aligned heart.

Even when I am nothing, I am breath and that breath is life.

I am life.

And if I am life, I am connected to all life. I am all, we are one.

When we are one, I am not alone.

To simply *be* is to exist in each moment, in the almighty everything that is nothing. When there is nothing, when the desires and needs are all stripped away, there is only the Source. Funny that when you remove all that is introduced in life and reach this nothingness, you are actually at the essence of being from which all was created.

The most powerful thing I have learned is what the Source actually is—that unfailing energy from which all was created, to which we are always connected.

I started to find my true Self by focusing on this element of who

I was, Source energy. I put my attention on being in the moment, on starting from nothing and observing how life unfolded in oneness. I eradicated the separateness that comes from judgment and comparative metrics of the swinging pendulum—adequate and unworthy, enough and insufficient, loved and irrelevant.

I am emotions, I am thoughts, and I am feelings. I am all of these things. When I take my focus away from them, I am stillness, and I am nothing.

When you strip away all the ways in which we are impacted, influenced, and shaped by our world, then we can rebuild it. Take it all away and start from nothingness and we become the choices we make in how we perceive and feel the world in each moment. Our happiness starts with uncovering our true Self via our authenticity.

SELF-ALIGNMENT THERAPY

One of the prominent nonmedical courses of treatment for depression, Cognitive Behavioral Therapy, was introduced by American psychiatrist Dr. Aaron T. Beck in the 1960s. It is a psycho-social intervention focused on negative thought patterns and overcoming dysfunctional cognitive distortions in thinking, behavior, attitudes, and emotional responses. It focuses on reframing thoughts and beliefs and introducing coping strategies.

Touching on that work and integrating everything we have learned so far, we now can look at Self-Alignment Therapy, a framework I developed that focuses on the coherence and alignment of emotions, thoughts, beliefs, and behavior in order to close the gap and pair both hedonic and eudaimonic happiness to experience healthy pleasure and life satisfaction.

5C Framework of Self-Alignment

- **Control** of emotions
- **Consciousness** of thoughts
- **Commitment** to beliefs
- **Continuity** of behavior
- **Consistency** of alignment

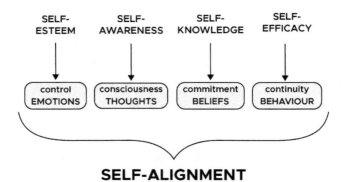

Diagram 5.1

Control of Emotions

I had just received an email from one of my girlfriends, Kar, who is definitely up there on the list of the hardest working people I know. We spent a year in high school together in Barbados when we were around fourteen years old, and then I moved to her homeland, the Netherlands, to do my university stint. She became one of the most focused, clear, and upbeat individuals I knew making it on the Next-Gen Under 30 list and so much more. I was understandably confused when I read this part of her email:

I really need to work on playing more,
even my doctor now pushes for it, as I am basically
not producing any female hormones at the moment
being suppressed by stress. Even though I don't
feel stressed, the body is a weird thing.

I was so baffled, as she really did seem like she was enjoying life and integrated a lot of adventure activities into it. I knew I had to revisit this whole topic of stress and found myself wondering if one could experience opposite emotions at the same time.

So that became a bit of an emerging theme: happiness/sadness, sickness/health, pain/pleasure, success/failure, stress/relaxation.

I like to call this my Theory of Opposites: the inability to experience two opposite thoughts or emotions simultaneously.

If you are ever in the dark, not quite able to pinpoint where your stress is coming from, then guess what, you may not need to figure it out. Sometimes all you need to do in the face of stress is to do things that will help you relax. There are times when I feel so happy in my mind that I do not understand that my physical body can be experiencing stress. Once I do a meditation, even just ten minutes of focusing on my breathing, it's amazing how much I can feel my body releasing that stress. Your Cognitive Self may not be able to pinpoint stress, but your Affective Self certainly can. We know it sometimes simply by feeling the absence of its presence when it is gone. We realize we were burdened only after we feel relief. Once again, you can see how the Executive Self takes the lead with action and your emotional response will change accordingly, and only then will you feel the difference.

Find the space between what you want and what your body needs. This is the space between desire and satisfaction.

If we act impulsively and go on a shopping spree to help de-stress and end up spending a fortune but are left with feelings of guilt, then the degree of satisfaction with our choice only stands to leave us feeling more stressed. I have tangoed with this cycle of numbing actions intending to help me relax only to leave me with some degree of guilt or regret. Having said that, it is subjective. I do go out and shop, buy a few items I absolutely love, while positively affirming that I am worth spoiling myself. I am grateful for the items I get or the sashimi and sake lunch I spontaneously enjoy. I treat myself well and compensate in other ways.

We can do a little budget maneuvering to eradicate the guilt of feeling financially aloof, superficially material, or impulsive in our purchases. At the end if we feel happy, we know we did something nice that helped us relax.

There are other scenarios, however, where we may go out and end up drinking tequila, singing at the top of our lungs with Svetlana, lost in the moment like free spirits, more and more rounds as the laughter gets louder. Oh the joy. Until the next day, when we see our bank account and think, *Wow, I really did not need all of those bottles or this hangover.* Did we really feel good? Would we choose to do it all over again?

Perhaps not.

Yet somehow we can find our Selves in that very cycle, repetitively doing things that do not leave us happy. The temporary numbness, temptations overindulged in, and a surplus of cognitive overwhelm, which now is stress with the addition of some bonus emotions.

We must **think** about what we truly **believe** will have the most

positive, emotional impact and **act in accordance** with that.

This is the art of alignment, the synchronicity of the Selves.

Emotions

Every emotion is *energy in motion* that is measured by a frequency, hertz.

The frequency is that to which all in our life attracts.

If we do not recognize what frequency we are on, we are not in control of what we are manifesting. If we are stuck on a low frequency because we have not developed emotional Self-awareness, I truly believe we cannot reach ultimate happiness. We have lightning bolts of emotional energy surging in our body, creating biological, psychological, and neurological reactions and counteractions. Are you aware enough to know what your emotional state is, and have you developed the intelligence to control those emotions?

Everyone experiences and perceives life via their mental and physical routines. There is no universal reaction or one-size-fits-all formula. We see the world as we are, not as it is. There are no standardized robotics built into the human species that control and predetermine our day-to-day behaviors. Sure, there is dancing the survival two-step of eating, working, sleeping, and repeating, but even those actions are done by choice. The phenomenon of emergent Self-knowledge is real.

The human hierarchy of needs motivates the choices we make, but if our actions are not predetermined concretely, then in each moment we have an opportunity to change our choices. In any given moment, you have the chance to act in ways driven by joy, to choose what feels euphoric, to choose alignment. You even have the choice to allow what feels less than joyful, to observe and recognize it, and work through those feelings instead of avoid, deny, or belittle them. Depression sets in when there is a consistent numbness to life, when we make our relationship with our feelings insignificant, when we allow our power to become dormant.

If our actions are not motivated to serve our happiness, what is driving us?

Purpose is to live with an intention and to be driven by a reason. I think joy should be that reason.

Our conscious devotion to every minute while awake leads to an extremely subjective encounter with life, whether that has become automated or stimulating. Each minute is different from the one before it, repetitively familiar in how time passes, yet unpredictable in the capacity of how we can choose to feel it. We can curate purpose through an intention of feeling.

Why you do anything you do is driven by what you desire to feel when you accomplish your goals. It would be sad to think that you have been conditioned to put your feelings outside the lens of importance when making your choices. Or worse, manipulated to value life milestones that actually don't leave you feeling anything that resembles authentic happiness.

Are you living in alignment with your purpose, or are you living with the intention to accomplish something that is actually the purpose of another individual or company?

It would be terrifying to think that we have been numbed into a bearably depressed state through a system that undervalues the importance of our purpose and individuality. The time is now, when the personal yearning for joy shall be unmuted, as tolerance finds its expiration and the life right to happiness is loud. Suppressing dissatisfaction only serves to widen your gap, so do not fear to speak up authentically to advocate for the deep life purpose you are yearning to fulfill.

The hope of liberation is to know the power of making your own feelings the highest priority. Embracing this life philosophy could change the course of your entire existence. Simply choose to shift from *them and their needs* to *me and my needs*, and discover the happiness of the individual Self as it transcends in aligned energy. It will naturally evolve into a desire to contribute to the connected whole. When you honor your authenticity, you will develop a desire to Self-actualize and be driven by meaning. Your contribution should not be from fear of reprimand or threat to survival, but rather from the joy of existing by living a purpose-driven life.

Imagine you started observing how you feel about all that comes from this moment forward. Your reason for action, your motivations, your reactions, your ability to find the significance in your choices.

Two people could undertake the exact same task, live the same lifestyle, and feel immensely different toward their individual lives.

What makes you who you are, is how you feel about what matters to you.

Can you truly epitomize who you are if you isolate your Self from the feelings that connect you with passion to your reason for living? Do you know the difference between unhappy and happy?

Here are ways to tell if you are unhappy:

- Unfavorable Self-image
- Tiredness, exhaustion, feeling depleted for no reason
- Unhealthy and frustrating relationships
- Loneliness
- Judgmental mentality
- Constant comparison

- Minimal job satisfaction
- Feeling undervalued or not feeling appreciated
- Lack of empowerment
- Uncertainty about your purpose in life
- Over-analyzing trivial decisions
- Talking about others, malicious gossip
- Making choices that are bad for your health and well-being
- Addictions to something negative while knowing you want to break that addiction
- Disappointments from unmet expectations and disgust with repeated try-and-fail behaviors

To be happy, we need to look at our past, present, and future.

The way we store memories from our past, perceive them in our present, and the way we hope to respond to life emotionally in the future all influence our happiness.

Memories can be recalled with the same emotional charge with which they were stored. This is why people with post-traumatic stress disorder (PTSD) feel like they are suffering the pain all over again, as if it were happening to them in the present. If the stimulus that initiated the trauma reoccurs (a trigger), the body can repeat the pain response that it originally felt. It helps to change the way in which the memory is stored by positive reinforcement, forgiveness, mindful perception, and perspective. I've found that trauma unhealed is one of the most disruptive things in life, and it's worth it to master control over past pain.

There is no possible way we can control every occurrence in our life, so it is logical to believe unresolved emotional trauma will be triggered. Life is lived fullest by feeling our emotions, even if that is via memory and recalling an experience or through completely new experiences. Studies that explore the impact of the brain when we think of happy memories and experience positive nostalgia found significant health benefits, like a more active prefrontal cortex linked to enhanced emotional regulation and cognitive control. Reminiscing about positive memories buffers acute stress responses, according to Speer and Delgado (2017). What was also really uplifting was reading that positive memory recall was also associated with reduced vulnerability to depression (Askelund, 2019).

Thinking about great times in the past is so good for us. It actually lessens stress and improves relaxation as cortisol, a stress hormone, is kept in balance. This goes hand in hand with feeling grateful for things that have happened to you and rewiring the brain to more pleasant states. On the flip side, there has also been findings that depression negatively impacts the brain and memory in ways that mimic the symptoms of dementia, what some call pseudodementia.

Emotions have so many implications beyond memory recall. In our present state, certain emotions activate our survival mode, especially if there is a feeling of fear, anxiety, or danger. Our system will assume we are under a threat of attack and activate this stress response, which is not problematic if only endured for the intended short term. However staying in negative emotional states for extended periods by not being honest about our feelings, not understanding emotions, expressing them, or taking the required action to change our emotional state actually keeps us in survival mode. Without returning to balance, this has serious health implications when sustained over the long term and hence, why stress got the name "the silent killer."

It is imperative to understand that the survival brain is resistant to change while the thinking brain serves a higher purpose and seeks growth. If we cannot move past our negative emotions, we cannot activate the part of the brain that affords us our greatest potential. Self-actualization requires the thinking brain to be in control, which can only be activated once a feeling of safety and positive emotional states are being met. You have to take control of your Affective Self and what it feels in order to ensure that your Cognitive Self and Executive Self can master happiness and life satisfaction.

The thinking brain is where we crave growth, where we move toward greater Self-development and achievement. Moving toward Self-actualization requires moving out of our survival (pain avoidance) Affective Self into our Cognitive and Executive Selves, where reasoning mode (pleasure-seeking) and satisfaction can be attained. More satisfaction and achievement should enhance motivation and increase the desire to reach greater states of fulfillment as you heard about in relation to the achievement drive in Chapter 3. Dopamine is released when you feel accomplished, and that builds your Self-esteem and Self-efficacy.

This is the power of emotional awareness. Without it, you are unknowingly being held captive in a state that encourages you to stay safe and comfortable. I once read a quote that said, "Comfort zones are nice, but nothing ever grows there." I cannot imagine building the life of your dreams without it requiring growth in some capacity, and growth requires change.

This critical step of actually acknowledging an emotion and choosing a response rather than an instinctive reaction is the difference between activating the survival brain or the thinking brain.

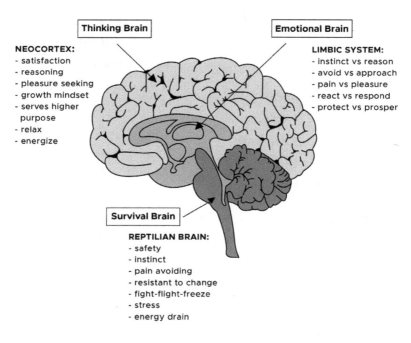

Thinking Brain

NEOCORTEX:
- satisfaction
- reasoning
- pleasure seeking
- growth mindset
- serves higher
  purpose
- relax
- energize

Emotional Brain

LIMBIC SYSTEM:
- instinct vs reason
- avoid vs approach
- pain vs pleasure
- react vs respond
- protect vs prosper

Survival Brain

REPTILIAN BRAIN:
- safety
- instinct
- pain avoiding
- resistant to change
- fight-flight-freeze
- stress
- energy drain

Diagram 5.2

The feeling we associate with an emotion and the meaning we give it will motivate our behavior to either protect our comfort zone or prosper with courage. There is a difference between reacting (instinct and impulse) and responding (reason and intention). Reactions are not all bad. Sometimes we react so quickly to situations, our reflexes save us from car accidents, tree branches, or tripping and falling flat on our face. The emotional distinction I want you to focus on is knowing what is constructive and what is destructive.

Destructive emotions are the low vibrational frequency of energy in motion and are associated with stress, which increases our pulse, releases adrenaline, and redirects our blood flow to major organs instead of extremities and releases a surge of hormones including cortisol. Cortisol provides the body with energy resources (glucose) to ensure our best chance of survival in the event of fight or flight. Too much cortisol in the body over the long term has been linked to:

- Increased appetite, causing weight gain
- Increased blood pressure
- Danger of osteoporosis
- Digestive issues
- Muscle weakness

It plays an important role in regulating our metabolism, immune system, and even memory formation. This stress hormone inhibits the immune system to a point that we are much more susceptible to colds, flus, and infections, which tip us off our game. I know that when I am stressed and I feel run down, it's not long before I realize my immunity is shot or my energy levels bottom out. Anyone suffering from issues impacting health will be a testament to how consuming it is to address these ailments. The distraction of working through these issues is not only burdensome, it's just downright draining. If you do not make time for your mental health, be prepared to make time for physical illness.

The Tipping Point of Courage

To understand emotions is to understand frequency and vibration.

The Solfeggio frequencies are electromagnetic sound vibrations used by Georgian monks as music tones while chanting meditatively. In 1974, these frequencies were further explored by Joseph Puleo in their capacity to influence the consciousness of humans to stimulate healing. A fascinating turning point in my exposure to frequency was looking at how these tones related to the emotional frequency of my life and how that created my vibration, or more simply put, my "vibe." They say our vibe attracts our tribe, but more than that, our vibration is what controls the law of attraction. It is the point to which all in our life will be attracted and manifested.

By controlling emotions, we can create new realities of existence.

The list of emotions and their corresponding frequency (Hz) are as follows:

Frequency	Emotion _Stimulus_
1000	God consciousness
900	**Gratitude, freedom, empowerment**
780	Appreciation
700	Enlightenment
600	Peace, serenity
540	Joy
500	Love, enthusiasm, happiness, positive expectation, belief
400	Reason, hope, optimism
310	Willingness
250	Neutrality, boredom
200	**Courage, frustration, irritation, impatience, overwhelm**
175	Pride, discouragement, blame, worry, resentment, doubt
150	Anger, hatred, rage
125	Desire, jealousy

100	Fear
75	Grief, loss, sadness, rejection, loneliness
50	Apathy, depression
30	Guilt, regret, insecurity, dishonesty
20	Shame, unworthiness, powerlessness, despair
0	Death

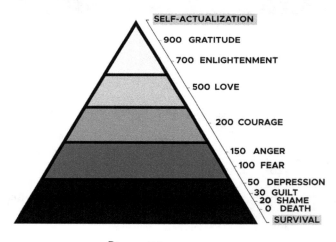

Diagram 5.3

I started to ask myself how we could narrow down emotions to the most basic categories, and I was able to deduce the following four: fear, anger, sadness, and happiness. I called these our surface-level emotions because we can easily identify with them, but I wanted to get to the root of their cause. The Solfeggio frequencies have been equated to the body's seven chakras, or energy centers, which are as follows:

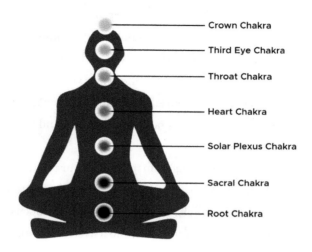

Diagram 5.4

As I started to decipher the Solfeggio frequencies, I noticed that getting to the root of emotions was often associated with the lowest listed frequencies on the chart, which ironically are hosted in the root chakra. I listed each of these, recategorized them, and dissected their meaning until the *eureka* moment hit. Almost all of them were associated with a feeling of loss. Loss of Self-worth (shame), loss of hope (despair/depression), loss of confidence (insecurity), loss of acceptance (rejection), and so forth. The feeling of rejection if you are familiar with it can be an incredible source of rage, loss of rationality, and desperation to fix the problem that led you to feeling rejected. It is not an emotional state that people often cope with easily, or can sustain its feeling for lengthy periods, which is why breakups can be so devastating.

Rejection is meant to feel that overwhelming because, while evolving, it was a danger to survival. Being ostracized from the tribe meant you were likely to be vulnerable to threat and could potentially face death. This would be a powerful stimulus requiring action to ensure survival. Humans evolved and now experience rejection in many ways. We sometimes believe that we are being rejected when we do not receive the desired validation, achievements, or affection we expect. The question is, are we aware of it and how does it influence our behavior?

Emotions may linger on to become our feelings and moods based on the thoughts we apply to them. These thoughts sometimes hinge on unrealistic beliefs, as we have previously discussed.

I continued to evaluate the most destructive emotions to the most constructive, and what I discovered is there is a tipping point that happens at around 200Hz with an emotion called courage. I started to focus more on courage over comfort zones, courage in the face of fear, courage to love, courage to pursue my purpose. It is my belief that the more you embody high-frequency emotions starting with courage, the higher your vibration will be. As you continue with momentum in higher vibrations by sustaining constructive positive emotions, you will evolve toward Self-actualization.

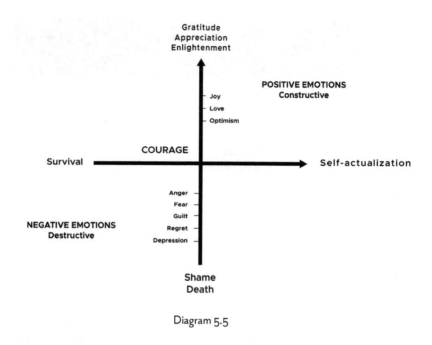

Diagram 5.5

Raising the Vibration

As most destructive emotions deal with some type of loss, we can apply the Theory of Opposites to counteract the feeling of loss. If we focus on regaining what was lost, we recover it. It seemed appropriate, putting this attention to healing our Selves under the umbrella of recovery. Think of recovery as regaining emotional control and healing your frequency.

Here is a summary of your chakra energy centers in your body, the frequency and emotions, how that relates to your brain, and the thoughts and feelings you can observe and evaluate for recovery.

Chakra / Emotional center	Frequency	Emotion	Brain	Thought/ Feeling
Crown	1000	God consciousness	**THINKING BRAIN:** (Neocortex) —relaxed state that is energizing	Pleasure-seeking
	900	**Gratitude, freedom, empowerment**		
	780	Appreciation		
	700	Enlightenment		
Third Eye	600	Peace, serenity		Reasoning mode focused on satisfaction
	540	Joy		
Throat	500	Love, enthusiasm, happiness, positive expectation, belief		Growth mind-set, thrive and serve higher purpose
	400	Reason, hope, optimism		
Heart	310	Willingness	EMOTIONAL BRAIN: (Limbic)— beliefs and values	Pain vs. Pleasure
	250	Neutrality, boredom		React vs. Respond
	200	Courage, frustration, irritation, impatience, overwhelm		Avoid vs. Approach

The Intelligence of Happiness

Solar Plexus	175	Pride, discouragement, blame, worry, resentment, doubt	SURVIVAL BRAIN: (Reptilian)— fight, flight, or freeze response/ stressed state that drains body	Pain avoidance
	150	Anger, hatred, rage		
Sacral	125	Desire, jealousy		Instinctive mode focused on safety
	100	Fear		
	75	Grief, loss, sadness, rejection, loneliness		
Root	50	Apathy, depression		Fixed mind-set, resistant to change
	30	Guilt, regret, insecurity, dishonesty		
	20	Shame, unworthi-ness, powerless-ness, despair		
	0	Death		

Diagram 5.6

Emotional Response Mechanism

Developing an Emotional Response Mechanism (ERM) is a way to integrate what you know now about your emotions and take control.

- **Identify** and name the exact emotions you are experiencing.
- **Explore** the surface to root of the emotion by utilizing curiosity and asking what could be causing this emotion. Ensure you feel authentic and nonjudgmental.
- **Pinpoint** what state of destruction is present in the root by identifying the area of loss.
- **Apply** the Theory of Opposites to illuminate the focus of recovery.
- **Decide** what constructive emotion is most beneficial to counteract the destructive.
- **Practice** courage to overcome the destructive and embody the constructive.
- **Enhance** this with an emotional antidote.

Emotional antidotes like *forgiveness* and *appreciation* allow us to transform destructive low vibrational frequencies that destroy our energy, health, mind, body, and soul, and instead facilitate the exact opposite of the fight-or-flight stress response. These antidotes induce the relaxation response, empowering a sense of control and reason instead of instinct. In opposition to protecting your comfort zone, they open the gateway to your prosperity and pleasure, and they ensure the gap can be closed by first understanding where it exists. What you think about your emotions matters just as much as being able to identify them.

Consciousness of Thoughts

As we evolve from our Affective Self and progress in intelligence, we become more aware of differing dynamics of happiness and its potential complexity. Thoughts play a role in this, and you will begin to understand how your consciousness serves your happiness.

Consciousness is a developed awareness that pairs the emotions and thoughts we have in our body and mind in ways that allow us to choose our feelings. Our consciousness dictates the perception phenomenon. It is the energetic space of consideration and deliberation before we allow our Self to settle snugly into how we feel about any given experience. To be conscious, we must be aware of our thinking and monitor both the quantity, quality, and the vibrational frequency of our thoughts and emotions in unison.

Every emotion is energy in motion, and that frequency then becomes a thought frequency as it is perceived. I can't say this enough, this combination of emotion and thought vibration is the point of attraction to which all else manifests itself. If you have negative thoughts, you exist on a lower vibrational frequency with destructive emotions and negative thinking. Quite the same, like will attract like, positive will attract positive.

Your reality is really just a physical realization of that which exists first as an energetic frequency in the form of emotion and thought.

Once you continue to think and feel a certain way, the powerful magnetism of that frequency held in duration amplifies the ways in which things unfold in your life. Hold your attention in awareness of your Self and ask, "How is my Affective Self serving that which I am trying to accomplish in life? Is it supporting my alignment to ensure happiness, pleasure, and satisfaction?"

Judgment and discrimination are parts of our Cognitive Self that allow us to apply logic and reason, and to use memory to create opinions from previous experiences. We can step back from assumptions and place our Self in a position of observation. Allow the world to be felt.

With delicate care, choose to feel and filter your emotions. You can then apply a constructive Emotional Response Mechanism that opts for pleasure rather than pain, that chooses to perceive through the lens of high-frequency feel-good emotions.

Connected Detachment

As you learn to observe your thinking, your emotions, and thereby your feelings, you can create some distance from that which you observe. This space is called nonattachment or detachment and is one of the most fundamental understandings of happiness and closing the gap that I have learned.

To be connected enough to our circumstances that we can be aware of them and feel them, yet detached enough to observe them objectively and navigate peacefully through any situation, is the essence of connected detachment. To authentically observe what exists and is experienced is to hold our Self in a space of honesty as to what we feel about it. This is the starting point of alignment. What you cannot control, you can simply observe and make sense of through constructive and positive thinking.

We cannot always control outcomes, but our reactions to circumstances can be controlled constructively.

When we let go of expectations and what we think life should be like, then we already narrow the Authenticity Gap of Happiness significantly. Expectations and beliefs play a huge role in our gap. Alongside this, when we choose to experience life fully from a place of trust and of connected detachment, then we close the remainder of the gap between expectation and experience.

To be connected is to feel truthfully and wholly what *is*.

To be detached is to not try to control the inevitable unfolding of life.

To be happy is to expect the best and then find the best in each experience as it happens.

You can appreciate pain in grief as a reflection of the great love that you would have lost. You can appreciate fear because without it, courage would not feel so empowering. You can appreciate failure, rejection, illness, and all of those things that seem unfortunate if you start thinking in ways that focus on the high vibrational side of the story, the one that focuses on why you can still be grateful, the lessons, and the resilience.

Mindfulness and Self-compassion allow things to be noticeable about how we truly feel. Through committed, conditioned thinking we can reach happier places of Self because we have the awareness to recognize what is holding us back.

If we do not apply mindful perception of our thinking, the thoughts that pop up here and there become thoughts that are repeated, and those become lasting thinking patterns and deep-rooted feelings. We may experience the pessimism or negativity bias from an instinctual level, but if those thoughts are not managed and counteracted to positive perception, then our personality becomes negative, our worldview and Cognitive Self become negative, and our Executive Self acts in alignment with those expectations and beliefs.

We have to both honor and control emotions and be conscious and constructive in thinking. The optimism of positive thinking is strengthened through repetition, much like all other positive plasticity of the brain. What we repeatedly do becomes our second nature.

What are some of the empowering, supportive, and loving thoughts you have had about yourself today, or this week?

Proceed with caution and be wary of allowing positive thinking to suppress negative and honest burden. You have to know how to identify real emotion and shift the feeling around the emotion in a way that processes the emotion, not simply denies or ignores it, masking it with positivity. Get to the root of your emotions and then progressively and vibrationally escalate little by little.

One technique that is powerful to elevate emotions is positive affirmations.

This is especially constructive dealing with the Affective Self when Self-esteem has been questioned or there is Self-doubt. Our Self-talk is the stream of unspoken thinking patterns that become our mental habits. As we spoke about earlier, Self-defeating mental habits are one of the leading causes of nonclinical depression, especially when these thoughts become irrational and lack logic or reason. To eliminate the despair and potential depression from this negative mindset, we can use affirmations and statements of optimism that generally challenge and eradicate negative Self-concepts.

Self-Affirmation Theory

Claude Steele (1988) introduced the Self-affirmation theory to address the Self-image of individuals who had been threatened as a means to affirm the integrity of the Self. In an effort to restore or in some cases maintain a strong Self-image, positive statements that position the individuals in a favorable and admirable light helped them overcome struggles with Self-image. I love affirmations and write them down in my journal pretty much every day, right after I write my blessings. Two of the most powerful words you can say are "I am," and then fill in the blank with something powerfully uplifting. I say them sometimes while in the shower, or staring into my own eyes in the mirror. I repeat mantras when I know I will be faced with challenges. It helps when we are alone, it helps when we are in society, it helps especially if we experience the psychological implications of cognitive dissonance where there is an inconsistent nature between our cognition and behavior.

Conflicting cognitions between our inner Self-talk and the beliefs of our peers can be overcome by affirmations rooted in acceptance, respect, and diversity.

I am accepting of different opinions.
I am respectful to others.
I am enjoying diversity.
I am able to resolve conflict easily.
I am open to different perspectives.
I am confident in my beliefs.
I am still loved despite differences in opinions.

If our thoughts and actions, however, are not aligned, that distress can impact any of the Self-concepts across the three Selves. Positive affirmations not only help to overcome such conflict, but also aid in encouraging the alignment of the Affective, Cognitive, and Executive Selves, which bridges the Authenticity Gap of Happiness. Such affirmative thinking powerfully places our emotions in a positive state, and as this is repeated, the brain's plasticity will restructure to the point that these affirmations are held as truth and become part of the Cognitive Self's belief system and our Self-knowledge.

It's the repetition of affirmations that lead to belief.
And once that belief becomes a deep
conviction, things begin to happen.

—MUHAMMAD ALI

Simply put, affirmations feel damn good. They almost immediately lead to happiness. The more regularly I practice them, the better. Affirmations activate the reward centers of the brain, especially the ventral striatum and ventromedial prefrontal cortex that is the keystone of Self-esteem and stimulates confidence and motivation. This will improve our productivity and also aid in improving our levels of Self-efficacy.

Some examples of affirmations include:

Affective

I am worthy.
I am enough.
I am an asset to the world.
I am virtuous.
I am kindness.
I am compassionate.
I am able to provide value.
I am confident in my worth.
I am feeling happy.
I am grateful.
I am appreciative.
I am Self-aware.
I am brilliant.
I am ambitious.
I am winning.
I am prosperous.

Cognitive

I am always learning.
I am intelligent.
I am getting better and better every day.

I am broadening my beliefs.

I am using my beliefs to support my goals.

I am a work in progress.

I am growth.

I am positive.

I am optimistic.

I am choosing wisely.

I am evolving in positive ways.

Executive

I am capable.

I am fueled by courage.

I am overcoming my fears.

I am facing challenges boldly.

I am a high-performing person.

I am discipline.

I am flow.

I am committed.

I am reliable.

I am consistent in my actions.

I am actualizing on my potential.

I am making a positive impact.

I call this Affirmative Neurocognitive Programming, because its benefits are so far-reaching, and this type of exercise programs my three Selves in such powerful ways that my cognition, psychology, and neurology are all immediately impacted. If you don't believe me, put this book down right now and start shouting some affirmations, or just whisper them.

Nothing works, however, if we do not commit to and believe in it.

Commitment to Beliefs

The power of beliefs really struck me deeply when I learned about the medical results of the placebo effect.

How could a pill with zero medicinal effect produce real biological results?

For centuries placebos have been used, whether physical, pharmaceutical, or psychological, and the substance with no proven medicinal implications somehow miraculously relieves symptoms. It's quite a noteworthy phenomenon, as documented in a Harvard Health Publishing article (Lambert, 2007), which commented on Ted Kaptchuk's study that found even when people knew they were taking the placebo, it was 50 percent effective.

To me, that is the power of belief.

If you truly believe that something will provide relief, that you will see results, and that you will be healed, then you most likely will.

The Phenomenon of Deception

The most intriguing in the phenomenon of deception is the psychological placebo. What the mind believes has the power to deceive the entire body. You can essentially start to believe in your ability to control your own health and happiness, and you will. From false statements to misleading information presented as truth, we shape our beliefs, and they impact everything from our emotions and thoughts right to our behaviors. Our beliefs are core to each of the three Selves.

The belief in the placebo effect, even while patients had the awareness that they were being treated with a placebo, still did not inhibit results. Further exploring the research of leading placebo expert, Ted Kaptchuk of Harvard Medical School, has shown that placebo treatments alter areas of the brain that regulate pain reception. This occurs even when patients are informed openly of the placebo—there are still meaningful therapeutic benefits.

If emotions and thoughts generate a frequency to which all else attracts and actualizes in reality, then beliefs have to be an even more powerful resource to shifting life satisfaction, pleasure, and happiness. If we train our Self with Affirmative Neurocognitive Programming, our beliefs will strengthen, and they will dictate what happens in our life.

So what are your beliefs?

Your emotions aid in showing you what you believe in. What you get aroused or angered by, what you find important when it comes to forming desires or goals, and similarly what you are satisfied by, and the types of accomplishments that matter to you, are all rooted in your beliefs. The beliefs you have in your worth or Self-esteem, the beliefs in your ability or your Self-efficacy, and even beliefs around your wisdom and Self-knowledge all play an important role in your life. Beliefs are the glue for our Self-concept and how we act in the face of those beliefs. In accordance with them or out of alignment with them contributes to our Authenticity Gap of Happiness.

It is therefore imperative to identify, reflect, and replenish our beliefs in accordance with our goals for life, our renewed understanding of happiness, and the journey ahead of pairing the two in long-term satisfaction.

As per Maslow's pyramid showing the human hierarchy of needs, we can evaluate the Self as it emerges toward Self-actualization and analyze the hierarchy of beliefs.

1. **Physiological.** Air, water, food, sleep, clothing, shelter, sex.

> *I believe that breathing and my relationship with air and oxygen enhance my life.*

Holding this belief would encourage me to do meditation focusing on the inhale and exhale, pace, and depth of my breathing. This belief gets me inspired to do breathing exercises like that of the infamous Wim Hof, because I believe in the impact and outcomes of these actions.

> *I believe that I can make healthy food choices easily.*

This belief programs my subconscious mind to crave healthy choices. Especially because I have conditioned the mind to find this easy, I can use this repeated thinking to condition my Self into the habit of healthy eating. It won't work if I simply do it out of the blue without care, emotional engagement, or the intention of it resulting in action. My beliefs need to be curated through thought repetition and Affirmative Neurocognitive Programming.

A thought becomes a belief once we hold that thought as truth.

Once I believe in this ability to make healthy food choices, my body follows that belief with action and association of ease.

If you believe and repeatedly think and speak about how you have no Self-control with your diet, that your cravings are intense, you will believe that, and it will continue to manifest as your reality. Change your thinking, change your language, and enhance the habitual inner dialogue that roots your Self in beneficial life-enhancing beliefs. There are several ways we can apply this approach to enhancing our beliefs in alignment with our psychological needs. We do it by simply looking at the statements below, gauging how we feel about them, associating high vibrational emotions and an optimistic mindset, and then repeating until the belief is empowered and life-enhancing.

For example, if you look at the statement, "I believe that I am attracting pleasure into my life," you might find that feels resistant, so you need to find out the root of that resistance. What does pleasure mean to you? Is it healthy pleasure, and how do you emotionally feel around these sources of pleasure?

Using your Emotional Response Mechanism, you can then say, "I actually feel shame, guilt, regret, pride, love, or gratitude in my sources of pleasure."

Example: guilty pleasures.

I believe that I am getting pleasure from junk food to numb my feelings of stress. I know I do not want to eat the things I eat, but I can't help myself.

- **Identify** and name the exact emotions you are experiencing.
  - ↪ Hostility, boredom, anxiousness
- **Explore** the surface to the root of the emotion by utilizing curiosity and asking what could be causing this emotion. Ensure you feel authentic and nonjudgmental.
  - ↪ Guilt, regret, shame
- **Pinpoint** what state of destruction is present in the root by identifying the area of loss.
  - ↪ Loss of Self-control, loss of discipline, loss of Self-worth, and loss of Self-esteem.
  - ↪ This stress eating makes me feel ashamed, and I lack Self-control and discipline with my food.
- **Apply** the Theory of Opposites to illuminate the focus of recovery.

- ↪ Recovery: feeling in control, taking control, knowing how to make the right choices at the right time
- ↪ Feeling worthy of health, believing discipline will do better by you than bingeing ever will
- **Decide** what constructive emotion is most beneficial to counteract the destructive.
  - ↪ Forgive yourself for your mistakes and bad choices previously.
  - ↪ Be grateful for your ability to start fresh using what you know.
  - ↪ Feel confident and courageous about eliminating junk food.
- **Practice** courage to overcome the destructive and embody the constructive.
  - ↪ I am strong enough to withstand the discomfort of cravings and withdrawals.
  - ↪ I am brave enough to face whatever underlying emotions might be driving me to Self-numb.
  - ↪ I am proud of my Self-awareness and efforts to address my weaknesses.
  - ↪ I am capable of overcoming challenges with grace and Self-love.
  - ↪ I believe that I can change my sources of pleasure to things that are healthier for me.
  - ↪ I believe I am capable, I believe in my Self, I believe I am improving my choices.
  - ↪ I believe that every day and every week I will see progress that brings me pleasure.
- **Enhance** this with an emotional antidote like forgiving your Self for previous failure and being grateful for your perseverance to try and finally get healthy.

This process of starting with your true, limiting, heavy, and false beliefs and seeing how they feel through the lens of authenticity is critical. You believe junk food relieves stress, but this is not a life-enhancing belief. You cannot resolve belief systems that are destructive if you do not get to the root of their emotional frequency, the truth of how they feel, and if they are defense mechanisms for much deeper-rooted feelings. You also cannot improve your life if you are negligent about your beliefs.

The progress comes from the process.

We must give our Self time to develop our Emotional Response Mechanism and vibrationally escalate as needed. One Self-aware step at a time; we will get there. We experience emotions first, and then we apply thinking to create how we feel, until eventually we will be able to shift our behavior.

Using constructive affirmations to reinforce positivity into cognition is essential. There is a reason why it has been repeated so many times throughout this book.

If you start to think in ways that justify your limiting beliefs, you will become a product of that limitation.

If you do not believe you can conquer, you will simply fail.

If you believe there is no way out of depression, you will stay in mental illness.

Start to look at all of your beliefs across all levels of your life. See if you can identify the Affective, Cognitive, and Executive presence in each. Then apply the Emotional Response Mechanism.

To kick off and touch on the other layers in the hierarchy of needs, I've provided some life-enhancing belief statements for stimulation.

2. **Safety and Security.** Personal, financial, health, and well-being.

I believe that I am safe.

I believe that the world I live in provides opportunities for my health.

I believe that I have access to things that enhance my well-being.

I believe that regardless of my finances I can make choices that invest in my health.

I believe that there is a lot of support for wellness.

I believe there are many activities that are free that help me stay healthy.

I believe that I have opportunities for financial abundance.

I believe there is an abundance of free resources that help me develop my skills and make me valuable to employers.

I believe that if I wanted to start my own business that I could find customers.

3. **Love and Belonging.** Friendships, intimacy, family.

I believe that everyone is deserving of love.

I believe that intimacy is a Self-enhancing feeling.

I believe that I have the capacity to love and be loved.

I believe that I can develop uplifting, supportive, and healthy relationships.

I believe that my attitude and accountability can help me build beneficial relationships.

I believe that I am a good friend and that I can always improve my friendship skills.

I believe that I have the ability to prioritize family.

I believe that I am willing to be honest about my needs in my relationships.

I believe that even if I am alone, that I will not be lonely.

I believe that the way I love myself teaches others how to love me.

I believe that no one can know me truly until I know my Self.

4. **Esteem.** Achievement, recognition, status, respect.

I believe that I can be proud of myself without needing external validation.

I believe that I can feel accomplished when I make an effort to do my best.

I believe that I can contribute value to the world.

I believe that I matter.

I believe that I am a work in progress and always improving.

I believe that I show respect to others.

I believe that effort breeds rewards.

I believe that I am worthy.

I believe that I have the capacity to make a difference.

I believe that living virtuous lives gains respect.

I believe that I can excel beyond my current status.

I believe that small wins are worth celebrating.

I believe that I am honorable.

5. **Self-actualization.** Realization of full potential, altruism.

I believe that I can become better than I am.

I believe that there are ways to innovate and improve.

I believe that challenge helps me excel.

I believe that I can learn more.

I believe that I have a purpose here on earth.

I believe that there is more to life than money.

I believe in making an impact in my community.

I believe in doing my part to live sustainably.

I believe that I am limitless.

I believe that I am Source energy.

I believe that I am powerful.

We can expand this exercise to include our societal beliefs as we navigate our mind to think about the positive and optimistic elements of society. Focus on the things that leave you feeling authentically appreciative of how society benefits your life. It is easy to find things to complain about, to criticize how this world falls short in abundance, but you become what you focus on. So wouldn't you rather give energy to the things that leave you energized?

You can think about the ways in which religion is good. If you are not religious, then activate your perception phenomenon and ask yourself if there are different perspectives to look at your belief system. Ask why you have the beliefs you have, why you can't allow multiple beliefs to hold truth while you commit to the ones that serve your own joy. Agree to disagree, because it's sometimes the pathway to happiness. Consensus is overrated. Choose to find different beliefs intriguing, passionate, and mind-expansive.

Life is not a one-size-fits-all template. Customize it to suit your authentic Self. Put your happiness and what brings you joy at the forefront while still allowing others to do the same. It's not a competition. Social comparison should not bring detriment and despair through constantly dividing us from our Selves and each other.

If there are situations or dynamics of society that anger you, you can still constructively use your Emotional Response Mechanism to identify what it is that angers you. Then you can apply an emotional antidote, find something to appreciate, or simply forgive others who have wronged you.

You will use a lot more energy and feel destroyed and depleted if you are pessimistic, negative, limiting, and obscene in your false beliefs. You just need to get out of your own fear of dreaming bigger, or feeling honestly what you feel, and just start perceiving your Self, your beliefs, and what you value as exactly what they are.

Be unapologetic in what matters to you.

The more you can learn about what is important to you, the more you can understand how your beliefs determine your motivations and your behaviors.

Limiting beliefs are those beliefs that limit our ability to reach a goal or actualize our own potential. They are rooted in internal perceptions of Self as well as the external ways in which we make assumptions about our environments and outcomes. They often are curated out of fear, lack of confidence, doubt, and sometimes subconscious assumptions that are Self-victimizing.

---

*"If you tell people your plans, they will steal your ideas."
vs. "I am creative enough to see my ideas through
with my unique perspective, and I know that when
I share these ideas that I can gain valuable insight
and enhance my strategy through feedback."*

---

*"You cannot trust that person—once a cheater
always a cheater." vs. "I know because that person
has cheated they must understand the dire consequences
and turmoil it causes. I also do not have to trust them.
I have to trust myself enough to be able to intuitively
and observantly tell if they are worth my trust.
I believe that I will make smart decisions
around who I give my trust to."*

> *"It's impossible to launch a successful*
> *product when the market is saturated with all the*
> *celebrity-branded products." vs. "The market is always*
> *promoting celebrity products when the majority*
> *of humanity is not celebrity status.*
> *So, there is an advantage and relatability that can*
> *be leveraged when you are part of the community*
> *and understand a customer's needs."*

A lot of the time we are not even fully aware of our limiting beliefs. Sometimes they are dressed as justifications and procrastination out of fear, or simply denial about our damaged Self-concept. These are the exact beliefs rooted in destructive emotions, negative mindset, and thereby low Self-esteem and low Self-efficacy. Often they will go hand in hand with emotions of unworthiness, rejection, and failure. Projection and deflection will also be right there in the presence of limiting beliefs.

> *"I am a failure" is different from*
> *"I failed at this one thing."*

> *"I am emotionally unavailable" is different*
> *from "I get emotional about my divorce."*

> *"I am too old" is the flip side to*
> *"I am wiser and more experienced."*

We see and hear these statements all the time. We affirm them and watch the evidence of them appear in alignment with our efforts to manifest them by thinking them, believing them, feeling them, and speaking them into existence.

It's too late in life to chase my dreams.
Switching careers is too hard.
I will seem unstable if I go after my dreams and fail.
There are never any interesting people around.
I am not understood, if people really knew me, I wouldn't be accepted.
I am hard to love.
I am not skinny enough to find a partner.
I am not rich enough to live in liberation.
I Self-sabotage and don't know why.
I tried my best and I am fine that it didn't work out.

Whatever our beliefs, they are loud, but first, we have to listen. To hear our screaming beliefs starts with engaging the heart of our Self-awareness, perception, and Self-compassion. Only then can we see how our behaviors are being driven and how to shift our beliefs to close the gap.

Continuity of Behavior

Of all the elements of Self, I would have to say the Executive Self is where I now place a majority of my energy. I can stay positive, grateful, and optimistic. I can believe good things will happen and that I have infinite intelligence and limitless potential. I can live in a visualized state of future manifestations feeling them as if they were my current reality. I have manifested things that have blown my mind and have done it time and again.

However, the one critical element I realize that makes that possible is **aligned action.**

We can all have the best intentions, but without action, nothing ever aligns. Taking action that is in alignment with your thoughts, beliefs, and emotional well-being is the keystone of closing the gap.

Every behavior we choose will result in a neuropsychological and neurochemical change in the brain and body. Our behavior literally changes our biology. It impacts our presence of neurotransmitters, our mood, and our ultimate feeling about life. We need to prioritize behavior, action, and continuity to stay in alignment. Tactically applying all that has been learned and understood in this book will do just that.

Controlling our emotions, being conscious of our thinking, and then committing to beliefs all come down to how we then transcend that knowledge from Affective via Cognitive into our Executive Self.

Without continuity, we won't practice the repetition that creates new positive plasticity. This is what we really need to focus on to form new powerful habits.

Repetition, continuity, doing the daily work.

You need to make a habit of choosing happiness. You need to make the effort to take action, to try and keep trying, because without the experience of aligned behaviors, you miss the chance to fully close the gap.

I repeat, you cannot close the gap if you do not take aligned action.

To incentivize yourself to act, try to use affirmations that support the desire to act. Use positive Self-talk to get started and stay focused on the feeling that you will have when you undertake the action. Once you behave the ways you know are best for you, the reward centers of the brain will indulge you with endorphins, dopamine, serotonin, and so many other delicious results of taking action.

Be mindful while taking action, celebrate effort, indulge in your learning and growth, and do not always hold your Self in judgment against expected outcomes. Connect to your experiences, detach from trying to control everything. Being totally present in my behavior and feeling how I live life, feeling my surroundings, feeling my body experience action is mind-blowing. When you really start paying attention, it is remarkable that you could have let so many things go unfelt, unnoticed, and brilliantly ignored.

I now feel the magnitude of life simply through my choice to be mindful.

Monitor your emotions and prioritize courage over comfort. Use your Self-awareness to identify fear. Invest in a healthy Self-efficacy. Use optimism and Self-esteem as leverage to get your Self going and keep going.

Continue. Repeat. Through action all resistance will be eliminated.

Much like when you tried riding a bike for the first time, or started a new job, went on a first date, or even cooked a new meal, after you have done it a handful of times, it's wired in the brain, and your neuroplasticity will support its continuity. It will become easier and will simply flow.

The interconnection between what we do and how it can make us feel was beautifully captured by William James, one of the fathers of American psychology, who said, "I don't sing because I'm happy; I'm happy because I sing."

Get out there, take action, and feel your choices. Learn to develop a relationship of awareness with your behaviors. Be courageous enough to fail, because you will still be learning and evolving, and the brain will still be engaged. The mind expanded. The horizons broadened.

The only way you can put your Self at a disadvantage is by only watching TV all day. It's the only leisure pastime that reduces brain function, dulls creativity, and lowers intelligence. Get away from the binge behavior of nonstimulating screen time. The only thing being stimulated is your dopamine addiction, and that will guarantee energetic depletion and payoffs of regret in abundance. Knowing the power of your emotions and that all is being attracted to that frequency, can you truly say you are willing to compromise your happiness because you simply are unwilling to dominate at better behaviors?

Find the balance of continuity to develop the ease of newly wired neurons and balance that with the infusion of unpredictability that helps the brain thrive and stay lively. You are not here to suffer or even just to sustain the struggle, but to thrive. Thrive and thrive and thrive to greater heights. Let your discipline be your desire. Let your reward be the action itself. Rewire your concept of indulgence to include courage, effort, progress, and action, and take great pride in your attempts.

The purpose of life is joy. Have fun.

The 5th C: Consistency

One of the things I have come to love is reading my statement of affirmative beliefs every morning. I usually do this after I journal and either before or after I meditate, depending on where I feel my alignment is.

Everything is always working out for me.

Everything supports my creative ideas materializing.

I have banished all doubts.

I am seeing evidence of my manifestations everywhere.

Everything is always working out for me.

I am nothing, even when I am nothing.

I am the whole universe being expressed in the power of my choice.

I am nothing, and even when I am nothing else, I am breathing and that breath is life, I am life.

I am all the brilliance of the universe manifested into this body.

Failure is the fun of discovering purpose.

Pain is showing me what I do not want out of life, I am learning.

Everything I have ever learned, I learned through repetition.

Progress is a process.

Do it with love or do not do it at all.

I am action, and the action is the reward, I am rewarded.

I see everyone as spirit, we are one.

I am vulnerability and vulnerability equals power, I am powerful.

I am unattached from expectation, to know that I can just simple BE, means I simply AM.

I am unconditional love.

I am Source energy.

I am infinite intelligence.

I am opportunity in each moment.

Now is all that matters, I start here, I start now.

I focus lovingly on the next best choice.

I am hope, optimism, and actualization.

I am healthy pleasure.

I am happiness evolving.

I am always having FUN.
THE PURPOSE OF LIFE IS JOY.

I wrote this at a very low point. It makes everything OK at all times starting with the statement "I am nothing." When I read it, I am always at ease, I tap into Self-love, I practice Self-compassion, I am unified with humanity and broken free from social comparison. I am perspective against the backdrop of the universe in its grandeur, I am but little, and in that I am relieved from the burden of desire for global recognition.

It does not all rest like giants anxiously panting on my shoulders when I am nothing.

I am simply and happily at ease.

When you write a statement like this, you know how helpful it is by how you actually feel when reading it. You should feel hugged by an adoring grandparent, you should feel powerful the way champions do, you should feel everything that is worth feeling in this life.

After reading my statement of affirmative beliefs, I am so high vibrational, confident, and bursting with gratitude that it is easy to jot down ten things I am grateful for. I write ten blessings and let them just pour out. When I skim over them, I make a point of feeling each of the key points in those blessings. I focus on my heart, sometimes placing my hand on my chest, activating my heart chakra and setting my vibration to feel gratitude in this energy center.

On the Solfeggio frequency chart, it is worth noting that gratitude vibrates at around 900 Hz, above enlightenment at 780 Hz. That's right, gratitude has a higher vibrational frequency than enlightenment, so now you can start to grasp the power of this emotion. I also truly believe the higher you vibrate, the closer you will be to Self-actualization as an all-encompassing state of hedonic and eudaimonic happiness and total life satisfaction.

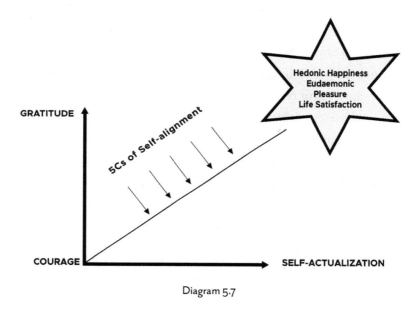

Diagram 5.7

It is worthwhile recapping just how powerful a few techniques are, which I call my Alignment Optimization Routine.

ALIGNMENT OPTIMIZATION ROUTINE
Meditation

Aside from the many neurotransmitters that are related to meditation and all those feel-good hormones that keep us relaxed, happy, and rewarded, when we consistently meditate, we thicken our prefrontal cortex and enhance the ability to regulate emotions and reason more clearly. Dara Lazar, a Harvard neuroscientist, found these correlations in her research and has advocated that the amount of meditation practice one undertakes will surely impact these benefits. The more experience the meditator, the more consistently they practice, the greater the rewards. Mindfulness meditations as well as kindness and gratitude meditations have time and again lit up brain scans in ways that now spotlight the science behind this spiritual practice. This is the most powerful thing that I have added into my routine to get into alignment. It is immediate, and I know how powerful and impactful it is, sometimes not by what I feel while meditating, but on the days that I have not done my practice and held space. It is with the highest and most encouraging recommendation that I say, get into it. Try and try again. The whole point, however, is not the effort to meditate, the resistance; it is the letting go and surrender of such force.

Where there is force there is no flow, and as Henry Ford said it best, "Whether you think you can, or you think you can't, you're right."

Journaling

Journaling is a technique that allows us to express an instant flow of consciousness and can be a method of Self-counseling. If you are not familiar with journaling, just write whatever comes to mind. Write in a book, or on your laptop, or on a piece of plain A4 paper. It does not have to be coherent, it does not have to be polished or grammatically correct, just write. This exercise has so many benefits with regards to processing emotional pain, being able to reflect, and even more so allowing one to recall positive memories, which as we talked about before, is quite happiness-inducing. The mere recollection of favorable experiences or relationships while journaling has immediate implications for your state of joy. Journaling even just for ten minutes every morning will help you feel satisfaction.

Write with the intention to enjoy it.

I personally also include my learning experiences and use it to find perspective. Especially when things are not going as I would hope, I tend to journal about what I can appreciate despite the unfavorable circumstances. I write my intentions in my journal every day. Sometimes this is just a sentence or two, but it helps me become very clear on what I want to get out of the day ahead. Reflecting has also been linked to increased performance as people have a chance to epitomize improvements through identifying what they would change and enhance in their future encounters. From purging pain, gaining perspective, and creating clarity, to inspiring intentions, and solidifying goals, the benefits of journaling are many. This creative technique is stimulating for the brain, and it can feel like pleasure. For me it feels like having an in-depth conversation with my best friend. It is personal, safe, and nonjudgmental. When I reach those points of unfolding fascination through journaling, I am beyond grateful for taking the time to do it. It always delivers.

The purpose of walking meditation is walking meditation itself. Going is important, not arriving. The same is true for Creativity. The same is true for journal writing. When you are in the flow of creation, you are here—going, walking, writing, but always here. The reason so many people block themselves from writing, from creating, is that they are not here. They have a head full of blueprints for the goal, they have elaborate outlines of how to get there, but they have never taken a conscious walk from their bedroom to their bathroom.

—BURGHILD NINA HOLZER

Affirmations

Reading my statement of affirmative beliefs daily is the kind of consistent action that gets me feeling like a superhero. I am not kidding, affirmations are the bootcamp coach you never asked for. You rewire your brain into believing that which you are affirming, and as you already know, you become what you believe. Writing or speaking affirmations or even just repeating them in your mind consistently will have huge impacts on your Self-esteem and Self-efficacy, making you more confident especially in your Executive functions. Affirmation, especially in a statement of upgraded and aligned beliefs, will shift and reshape your Self-knowledge and enhance the state of your Cognitive Self. These statements increase hopefulness, reduce stress, and all around feel rewarding. Use them to get motivated, increase productivity, or just move from suffering into struggling by affirming your power and control over your happiness.

I am capable of improving my emotions.

I can take control of my life.

I deserve happiness.

I am talented.

I am fearless.

I am disciplined.

I am patient and am making progress every day.

I am powerful.

I know I can fail and still keep going.

I am always able to improve.

I am capable beyond measure.

I am determined.

I am capable of extraordinary things.

I am supported.

I am loved.

I am worthy.

I am doing my best.

I know I have the universe on my side.

Things are not as bad as they seem.

I am grateful for all the things that are working out for me.

I feel excited about all the amazing things ahead.

I am delivering exceptional value.

I am winning in small and significant ways.

Consistency will breed rewards.

Much like the earlier sections, you can curate your affirmations to cope with whatever part of your life may need that extra assistance. I believed in my ability to become a millionaire, and so I said that affirmation with belief. I went to town on some Affirmative Neurocognitive Programming and it was fruitful. We all have to start somewhere, so be wary not to stretch your affirmation so far that you feel resistance. Much like vibrational escalation of emotions, escalate in your affirmations in alignment with your beliefs. You believe what you repeat. Remember, consistency is conditioning.

Gratitude

Writing my blessings and feeling grateful is one way to tap into the benefits of gratitude. You can also just observe life and feel grateful. You can say, "I am grateful for . . ." There are no confinements to the many ways in which you utilize gratitude for your benefit. They say you get more of what you are grateful for. So once you start to believe that and see the results that stem from this belief, I have a feeling you will be using gratitude a lot more than you currently anticipate. To be honest, when I first open my eyes in the morning, I have trained myself to think about what I am grateful for, even before my feet touch the floor.

> *I am grateful for the rest that has rejuvenated my body.*
> *I am grateful for the comfort, coziness, and safety of my bed and home.*
> *I am thankful for coffee, how it enhances my clarity and alertness.*
> *I am so so so thankful that my loved ones are safe and healthy.*
> *I am grateful I have work to awaken to that affords me my lifestyle.*
> *I am grateful that I still have a job.*
> *I am grateful the world is innovating and new opportunities are always unfolding.*
> *I am grateful for my Self-awareness and ambition.*
> *I am grateful for my new habits.*
> *I am hopeful about life.*
> *Thank you, thank you, thank you for my vitality to greet the day.*
> *It's amazing how energizing it can be, and that vibration gets you jumping into the day, positively empowered.*

You want to be consistent in your alignment. You want to ensure that you are controlling emotions, conscious of your thinking, committed to your beliefs and continuing to choose behavior that supports your alignment.

A FEW RULES OF HAPPINESS

Do Not Dwell—It Will Be a Great Disservice

Life is thickly sown with thorns,
and I know no other remedy than to
pass quickly through them.

The longer we dwell on our misfortunes,
the greater is their power to harm us.

—Voltaire

Do not entertain thoughts that are out of alignment. Every set of energetic resources you use to feel an emotion, to think a negative thought, is energy depleted. On the contrary, every powerful, high vibrational emotion and thought you feel energizes you. You will drain your Self in procrastination and destructive analysis until you break if you let your mind focus on the wrong things. Do not dwell. Choose wisely. If you have something happen that is upsetting, process it using your Emotional Response Mechanism, vibrationally escalate, and vibe high. Make vibrational elevation a habit, be consistent, keep the routine of getting your Affective Self to the happiest place you possibly can.

Self-Awareness Is a Weapon—Use It

> *We feel distress instead of eustress when we*
> *perceive something to be a threat*
> *rather than a challenge.*
>
> —TEAL SWAN

Filter and be fierce in the ways in which you distill the toxins of your mind.

There will always be stress, and as Austrian biochemist Hans Selye brilliantly differentiated back in 1936, "You can separate your stress into good stress, eustress and the bad kind, distress." Allow your Self to feel the stress of discomfort while you change. The sooner you accept it, the better you will be for it. Feel the eustress of laying the bricks that build the bridge and finally close the gap, but know that it's different from the low vibrational stress response of fight or flight. You have to realize that life will always breed something of stimulation in emotions you would rather not endure, but it is your ability to identify those emotions and change them. That is your power, and that power begins with Self-awareness. The buck stops with you.

Cognitive Restructuring Is Your Responsibility— Do It As Much As You Need To

> *But the whole point of liberation is that you get out.*
> *Restructure your life. Act by yourself.*
>
> —JANE FONDA

The Intelligence of Happiness

If you feel resistance, feel it. Decipher it. Listen to your Self and hear what beliefs are supporting that mindset, that discomfort, that lack of alignment. Be responsible with your mind and approach everything with a curiosity to understand what is widening the gap and what is helping to close it. You have to be consistent in this because it is quite the task to undo your lifetime of conditioning and mental structures. Use the versions of Self to make Self-analysis more niche. Laser focus with intention to discover more about your Self-knowledge and Cognitive Self. Hear the story you are telling your Self. What is your inner dialogue? What is your language to others?

Cognitive restructuring is a process of identifying and disputing thoughts that are maladaptive and distorted. Use this psychotherapeutic technique to become cognizant of your reasoning, your beliefs, generalizations, or exaggerations. Question them, apply alternative perspectives, expand your intellectual understanding.

Flow with the Changes

Change brings faster results
than chance.

—Amit Kalantri

You know that Darwin was the godfather of "survival of the fittest," and while you want to move beyond survival into Self-actualization, you need to ensure the Executive Self is changing with the changes. Every single experience contributes to the brain's plasticity. It impacts the Affective and Cognitive Selves each and every time you have a feeling, process it, and store it as memory or intelligence. You need to be mindful, present, adaptive, and invested in the ways in which you are perceiving life. You have the power to continue behaviors that will create new dominant neuropathways and habits, but life is not predictable. You have to be able to improvise, to seek out the locus of control, and still conquer in situations of the unforeseen.

Fail to plan and plan to fail, but if you fail to adapt, you will be unable to evolve.

Train your Executive Self to be open to the unknown and value your Self-efficacy to cope with any situation. Perform in ways that safeguard your alignment. Master the art of new mindsets, which only develop in the now. You evolve as you act, as you execute, as you elevate.

Value Progress as a Profound Element of Self-Actualization

> *I am a slow walker, but*
> *I never walk back.*
>
> —ABRAHAM LINCOLN

I know that this is just the first toe-dipping into the watering hole of solving the world's mental health crisis, but it's a start. I have learned that valuing progress is better than not making any effort. The topic of neuroscience used to intimidate me, until I read a book, then did some online courses and that overwhelm shifted. Over consistent commitment to learning, things became familiar. I started to connect the dots, and with time, I made some progress. It's OK to be a work in progress rather than the best thing since sliced bread.

Use purpose, leverage your achievement, drive to step right up to challenges, and let your courage be greater than your fear. Let failure be a learning curve you can laugh about in amazement as a mere step-ping stone. Enjoy the process of becoming your happiest Self. You know how to dominate and tap into your neurotransmitters to keep you in a state of pleasure as you shine bright and retreat in dimness, fall flat, and inevitably regroup. Stimulate the mind, brain, and body to keep in flow.

CONCLUSION

My favorite color has always been white.

I guess I was one of those people who thought, why choose when you can have it all. I had read that in order to get the color white, you actually need a spectrum of all the colors to combine.

You needed the whole rainbow, in its rare capacity of all elements coming together, much like I have learned why each technique in this book has colored my life with an unfailing ability to close my Authenticity Gap of Happiness, find my joy, and soar to new heights of success.

I find it a little ironic.

I put my whites into the washing machine, thankful for the bleach that redeems their distinguished bright and lustrous state.

The bleach I now hold is a beacon of transformative utility. From tainted to unsoiled.

I hold the bottle like a wartime grenade, something of historical significance, yet disarmed in its ability to cause havoc.

There is nothing like suffering to praise relief. There is nothing like a broken heart that affords you the enrichment of feeling its fullness once again.

I have been to so many places inside my soul, and many of them might be where you are right now, or where you could end up. I have suffered, I have struggled, and I continue to thrive. I have made my way through the war and have the souvenirs and scars that rest under the guardianship of my tamed demons.

I am in total control. I unequivocally declare, "There is nothing I nor you can't handle." Say it with me, "There is nothing I cannot handle."

The secret to life is the superiority of alignment across the three Selves: Affective, Cognitive, and Executive. They are like a tripod. All are necessary to stay standing balanced in your glory. Once you understand to execute on your 5C Framework of Self-Alignment, you will win at life:

1. Control over emotions
2. Consciousness of thoughts
3. Commitment to life-enhancing beliefs
4. Continuity of behavior
5. Consistency of that alignment

Abundance does not require haste, it requires alignment.

You are amazing. You got to the end of this book. You are a winner already simply because you have what most of humanity is yet to package up—an Alignment Optimization Routine that taps into the all-powerful techniques of meditation, journaling, affirmations, and gratitude. All simple, all destined to deliver results that you cannot begin to imagine.

When the tides change, adapt and enjoy the ride. You will continue onward and upward, because that's what people who read books like this do. They persevere by any means necessary.

Now, you will know happiness, and you will know your Self. Let the two be paired eternally in the power of authenticity and alignment.

Dancing on the air molecules of every breath to enter your lungs.

Live to love another day.

Fear not any breaking of your progress, and know that breaking down sometimes is breaking through.

Dine with your demons, serve them a can of whoop ass.

Clear any lingering emotional trauma that is holding you anchored from rising to your own Self-actualization.

Sit with your Self, now, ready, willing to do the work.

Knowing is not enough,
we must apply.
Willing is not enough,
we must do.

—BRUCE LEE

Your mind is equipped with the ammunition of optimism, perspective, appreciation, and forgiveness. Encounters that come to test you are merely part of your growth and an opportunity to demonstrate courage.

Smile.

Step boldly forward into challenge with eyes staring straight into life's hard choices.

Wink.

You are fearless.

Know, embody, and choose to perceive life in ways that leave you undefeatable.

The faith that surges in every molecule of my body leaves me with nothing short of certainty that you will, with consistent aligned action, live the most exceptionally impactful life.

Welcome to happiness, welcome to alignment.

REFERENCES

Self-Affirmation Theory. *International Encyclopedia of the Social Sciences*. Retrieved June 01, 2021, from https://www.encyclopedia.com/social-sciences/applied-and-social-sciences-magazines/self-affirmation-theory.

Alcaro, A., Carta, S., & Panksepp, J. (2017). The Affective Core of the Self: A Neuro-Archetypical Perspective on the Foundations of Human (and Animal) Subjectivity. *Frontiers in Psychology, 8*. https://doi.org/10.3389/fpsyg.2017.01424.

Armenta, C., Bao, K. J., Lyubomirsky, S., & Sheldon, K. M. (2014). Is Lasting Change Possible? Lessons from the Hedonic Adaptation Prevention Model. In K. M. Sheldon & R. E. Lucas (Eds.), *Stability of Happiness* (pp. 345–359). Elsevier. https://doi.org/10.1016/b978-0-12-411478-4.00004-7.

Armenta, C. N., Fritz, M. M., & Lyubomirsky, S. (2017). Functions of Positive Emotions: Gratitude as a Motivator of Self-Improvement and Positive Change. *Emotion Review, 9*(3), 183–190. https://doi.org/10.1177/1754073916669596.

Askelund, A.D., Schweizer, S., Goodyer, I.M. *et al.* (2019). Positive memory specificity is associated with reduced vulnerability to depression. *Nat Hum Behav 3*, 265–273. https://doi.org/10.1038/s41562-018-0504-3.

Balthazart, J., & Ball, G. F. (2006). Is brain estradiol a hormone or a neurotransmitter? *Trends in Neurosciences, 29*(5), 241–249. https://doi.org/10.1016/j.tins.2006.03.004.

Barker, E. (2016, February 28). Neuroscience of Happiness: 4 Rituals That Make You Happy. *The Week*. https://theweek.com/articles/601157/neuroscience-reveals-4-rituals-that-make-happy.

Bergeisen, M. (2019, September 22). The Neuroscience of Happiness. *Greater Good Magazine*. https://greatergood.berkeley.edu/article/item/the_neuroscience_of_happiness.

Breazeale, R. (2013, February 19). The role of the brain in happiness. *Psychology Today*. https://www.psychologytoday.com/intl/blog/in-the-face-adversity/201302/the-role-the-brain-in-happiness?quicktabs_5=1.

Brickman, P., Coates, D., & Janoff-Bulman, R. (1978). Lottery winners and accident victims: Is happiness relative? *Journal of Personality and Social Psychology, 36*(8), 917–927. https://doi.org/10.1037/0022-3514.36.8.917.

Cantril, H. (1965). *The pattern of human concerns*. Rutgers University Press.

Cerretani, J. (n.d.) The Contagion of Happiness. *Harvard Medicine*. https://hms.harvard.edu/magazine/science-emotion/contagion-happiness.

Duval, S. & Wicklund, R. A. (1972). *A theory of objective self awareness*. Academic Press.

Egan, O. (1986). The Concept of Belief in Cognitive Theory. In L. P. Mos (Ed.), *Annals of Theoretical Psychology* (pp. 315–350). Springer US. https://doi.org/10.1007/978-1-4615-6453-9_23.

Erozkan, A., Dogan, U., & Adiguzel, A. (2016). Self-efficacy, Self-esteem, and Subjective Happiness of Teacher Candidates at the Pedagogical Formation Certificate Program. *Journal of Education and Training Studies, 4*(8). https://doi.org/10.11114/jets.v4i8.1535.

Eurich, T. (2018). What Self-awareness really is (and how to cultivate it). *Harvard Business Review*. http://thebusinessleadership.academy/wp-content/uploads/2019/08/What-Self-Awareness-Really-Is-and-How-to-Cultivate-It.pdf.

Fennell, M. J. V. (1997). Low Self-Esteem: A Cognitive Perspective. *Behavioural and Cognitive Psychotherapy, 25*(1), 1–26. https://doi.org/10.1017/s1352465800015368.

Fernandez, A. (2014, July 7). Top 15 Insights About Neuroplasticity, Emotions and Lifelong Learning. *Huffpost*. https://www.huffpost.com/entry/top-15-insights-about-neu_b_5269699.

Fields, E. C., Weber, K., Stillerman, B., Delaney-Busch, N., & Kuperberg, G. R. (2019). Functional MRI reveals evidence of a self-positivity bias in the medial prefrontal cortex during the comprehension of social vignettes. *Social Cognitive and Affective Neuroscience, 14*(6), 613–621. https://doi.org/10.1093/scan/nsz035.

Fleming, S. M., Huijgen, J., & Dolan, R. J. (2012). Prefrontal Contributions to Meta-cognition in Perceptual Decision Making. *Journal of Neuroscience, 32*(18), 6117–6125. https://doi.org/10.1523/jneurosci.6489-11.2012.

Furman, D. J., Hamilton, J. P., & Gotlib, I. H. (2011). Frontostriatal functional connec-tivity in major depressive disorder. *Biology of Mood & Anxiety Disorders, 1*(1). https://doi.org/10.1186/2045-5380-1-11.

Hanson, J. L., Knodt, A. R., Brigidi, B. D., & Hariri, A. R. (2017). Heightened con-nectivity between the ventral striatum and medial prefrontal cortex as a biomarker for stress-related psychopathology: understanding interactive effects of early and more recent stress. *Psychological Medicine, 48*(11), 1835–1843. https://doi.org/10.1017/s0033291717003348.

Heid, M. (2019, December 5). The Power of Positive Memories. *Elemental*. https://elemental.medium.com/the-power-of-positive-memories-86c2441ffe07.

Henderson, L. W., Knight, T., & Richardson, B. (2013). An exploration of the well-being benefits of hedonic and eudaimonic behaviour. *The Journal of Positive Psychology, 8*(4), 322–336. https://doi.org/10.1080/17439760.2013.803596.

Hilbert, S., Goerigk, S., Padberg, F., Nadjiri, A., Übleis, A., Jobst, A., Dewald-Kaufmann, J., Falkai, P., Bühner, M., Naumann, F., & Sarubin, N. (2018). The Role of Self-Esteem in Depression: A Longitudinal Study. *Behavioural and Cognitive Psycho-therapy, 47*(2), 244–250. https://doi.org/10.1017/s1352465818000243.

Hofmann, S. & Asmundson, G. (Eds.) (2017). *The Science of Cognitive Behavioral Therapy* (1st ed.). Academic Press.

Hölzel, B. K., Carmody, J., Vangel, M., Congleton, C., Yerramsetti, S. M., Gard, T., & Lazar, S. W. (2011). Mindfulness practice leads to increases in regional brain gray matter density. *Psychiatry Research: Neuroimaging, 191*(1), 36–43. https://doi.org/10.1016/j.pscychresns.2010.08.006.

Huta, V. (2016). An overview of hedonic and eudaimonic well-being concepts. In L. Reinecke & M. B. Oliver (Eds.). *The Routledge handbook of media use and well-being* (pp. 14-34). Routledge.

Ikarashi, A. (2015, November 20). The search for happiness: Using MRI to find where happiness happens. *Eurek Alert!* https://www.eurekalert.org/pub_releases/2015-11/ku-tsf111915.php.

Joseph, S. (2017). *Authentic: How to be yourself and why it matters.* Piatkus.

Joseph, S. (2019, January 2). What Is Eudaimonic Happiness? How and why positive psychologists are learning from Aristotle. *Psychology Today.* https://www.psychology today.com/us/blog/what-doesnt-kill-us/201901/what-is-eudaimonic-happiness.

Judge, T. A., Bono, J. E., Erez, A., & Locke, E. A. (2005). Core Self-Evaluations and Job and Life Satisfaction: The Role of Self-Concordance and Goal Attainment. *Journal of Applied Psychology, 90*(2), 257–268. https://doi.org/10.1037/0021-9010.90.2.257.

Lambert, C. (2007, January-February). The Science of Happiness. Psychology explores humans at their best. *Harvard Magazine.* https://harvardmagazine.com/2007/01/the-science-of-happiness.html.

Lazar, S. W., Kerr, C. E., Wasserman, R. H., Gray, J. R., Greve, D. N., Treadway, M. T., McGarvey, M., Quinn, B. T., Dusek, J. A., Benson, H., Rauch, S. L., Moore, C. I., & Fischl, B. (2005). Meditation experience is associated with increased cortical thickness. *NeuroReport, 16*(17), 1893–1897. https://doi.org/10.1097/01.wnr.0000186598.66243.19.

Linden, D. J. (2011, September 6). The Neuroscience of Pleasure. *Huffpost.*

Maslow, A. H. (1943). A theory of human motivation. *Psychological Review, 50*(4), 370–396. https://doi.org/10.1037/h0054346.

McLachlan R. S. (2009). A brief review of the anatomy and physiology of the limbic system. *The Canadian Journal of Neurological Sciences. 36* Suppl 2, S84–S87.

McLeod, S. A. (2015). Freud and the unconscious mind. *Simply Psychology.* https://www.simplypsychology.org/unconscious-mind.html.

Melamed, L. E., & Melamed, E. C. (1985). Neuropsychology of Perception. In J. M. Adams & W. H. Jones (Eds.), *The Neuropsychology of Individual Differences* (pp. 61–91). Springer US. https://doi.org/10.1007/978-1-4899-3484-0_4.

Nafstad, H. E. (2015). Historical, Philosophical, and Epistemological Perspectives. In S. Joseph (Ed.), Positive Psychology in Practice (pp. 7–30). John Wiley & Sons, Inc. https://doi.org/10.1002/9781118996874.ch2.

Oonishi, S., Hori, S., Hoshi, Y., & Seiyama, A. (2014). Influence of Subjective Happiness on the Prefrontal Brain Activity: An fNIRS Study. In W. E. Crusio, H. Dong, H. H. Radeke, N. Rezaei, O Steinlein, & J. Xiao (Eds.), *Advances in Experimental Medicine and Biology* (pp. 287–293). Springer New York. https://doi.org/10.1007/978-1-4939-0620-8_38.

Ortiz-Ospina, E. & Roser, M. (2017, May). Happiness and Life Satisfaction. *Our World in Data*. https://ourworldindata.org/happiness-and-life-satisfaction.

Owen, S. F., Tuncdemir, S. N., Bader, P. L., Tirko, N. N., Fishell, G., & Tsien, R. W. (2013). Oxytocin enhances hippocampal spike transmission by modulating fast-spiking interneurons. *Nature, 500*(7463), 458–462. https://doi.org/10.1038/nature12330.

Pelusi, N. (2006, June 9). Removing Despair from Depression. *Psychology Today*. https://www.psychologytoday.com/intl/articles/200309/removing-despair-depression

Pennock, S. F. (2019, February 11). The hedonic treadmill — Are we forever chasing rainbows? *Positive Psychology*. https://positivepsychology.com/hedonic-treadmill/.

Perceptual Experience and Perceptual Justification. (2015, June 17). *Stanford Encyclopedia of Philosophy*. https://plato.stanford.edu/entries/perception-justification/#PerPhe.

Pessoa, L., & Hof, P. R. (2015). From Paul Broca's great limbic lobe to the limbic system. *Journal of Comparative Neurology, 523*(17), 2495–2500. https://doi.org/10.1002/cne.23840.

Qiu, L., Su, J., Ni, Y., Bai, Y., Zhang, X., Li, X., & Wan, X. (2018). The neural system of metacognition accompanying decision-making in the prefrontal cortex. *PLoS Biology, 16*(4), e2004037. https://doi.org/10.1371/journal.pbio.2004037.

Quoidbach, J., & Dunn, E. W. (2013). Give It Up. *Social Psychological and Personality Science, 4*(5), 563–568. https://doi.org/10.1177/1948550612473489.

Rudolph, L. M., Cornil, C. A., Mittelman-Smith, M. A., Rainville, J. R., Remage-Healey, L., Sinchak, K., & Micevych, P. E. (2016). Actions of Steroids: New Neurotransmitters. *The Journal of Neuroscience, 36*(45), 11449–11458. https://doi.org/10.1523/jneurosci.2473-16.2016.

Ryan, R. M., & Deci, E. L. (2001). On Happiness and Human Potentials: A Review of Research on Hedonic and Eudaimonic Well-Being. *Annual Review of Psychology, 52*(1), 141–166. https://doi.org/10.1146/annurev.psych.52.1.141.

Shenal, B. V., Harrison, D. W., & Demaree, H. A. (2003). *Neuropsychology Review, 13*(1), 33–42. https://doi.org/10.1023/a:1022300622902.

Shrestha, P. (2017, November 17). Skinner's theory on Operant Conditioning. *Psychestudy*. https://www.psychestudy.com/behavioral/learning-memory/operant-conditioning/skinner.

Sowislo, J. F., & Orth, U. (2013). Does low self-esteem predict depression and anxiety? A meta-analysis of longitudinal studies. *Psychological Bulletin, 139*(1), 213–240. https://doi.org/10.1037/a0028931.

Speer, M. E., & Delgado, M. R. (2017). The unfairness of being prosocial. *Nature Human Behaviour, 1*(10), 711–712. https://doi.org/10.1038/s41562-017-0222-2.

Spinelli, M. G. (2000). Effects of Steroids on Mood/Depression. In R. A. Lobo, J. Kelsey, & R. Marcus (Eds.), *Menopause* (pp. 563–582). Elsevier. https://doi.org/10.1016/b978-012453790-3/50040-8.

Spoon, M. (2018, February 16). New approaches in neuroscience show it's not all in your head. *News*. https://news.wisc.edu/davidson-talk-2018/.

Witters, D. & Harter, J. (2020, May 8). Worry and Stress Fuel Record Drop in U.S. Life Satisfaction. *GALLUP*. https://news.gallup.com/poll/310250/worry-stress-fuel-record-drop-life-satisfaction.aspx.

Worrall, S. (2018, March 17). Why the Brain-Body Connection Is More Important Than We Think. *National Geographic*. https://www.nationalgeographic.com/news/2018/03/why-the-brain-body-connection-is-more-important-than-we-think/.

CPSIA information can be obtained
at www.ICGtesting.com
Printed in the USA
BVHW092213160921
616890BV00010B/1007/J